WILD HAIR

A COURAGEOUS WOMAN'S GUIDE
TO A BOLD AND AUTHENTIC CAREER

WILD HAIR

A COURAGEOUS WOMAN'S GUIDE TO A BOLD AND AUTHENTIC CAREER

TRACY J. EDMONDS

Niche Pressworks
Indianapolis

For permission to reprint portions of this content or bulk purchases, contact Tracy J. Edmonds at TracyJ@TracyJEdmonds.com.

ISBN-13: paperback   978-1-952654-15-2
ISBN-13: hardback   978-1-952654-16-9
ISBN-13: eBook   978-1-952654-14-5

Published by Niche Pressworks, Indianapolis, IN
http://NichePressworks.com

Printed in the United States of America

AUTHOR'S NOTE

It's a privilege to be a coach. I've had the opportunity to coach many wonderful women who entrusted me with their deepest thoughts and concerns during their careers. As their trusted advisor, confidentiality is my top priority. There is no coaching relationship without it.

I believe in the power of story. Stories connect. They inspire. They teach. In the spirit of lifting other women, I've told my stories and the stories of those I've coached to the best of my recollection. To protect confidentiality, I have changed names, roles, titles, industries, and any other potentially identifying characteristics.

DEDICATION

Dedicated to my mother, Shirley Jackson.
Whenever I was lost or questioned what I should do, she always
replied, "Just be you, Tray."

ACKNOWLEDGMENTS

I'd like to thank my family—husband Anthony, daughters Devan and Alynne, and son Adrian—for taking this wild ride with me, encouraging me every step of the way, and putting up with the long hours that I was locked away in our office, banging on the laptop keys.

Thank you to my personal coach, Dena Patton, who kept me focused on my greatness throughout this journey.

Thank you to my editors, Anna Flynn and Julie Salzmann, at Heartland Prose, whose feedback was always uplifting and honest to help me write the best book possible.

Thank you to Nicole Gebhardt and the staff at Niche Pressworks for guiding me through the publishing process.

Thank you to my best friend, Teresa L. Thomas, who always said I had stories to tell and never doubted that I'd make my dream to write a book come true.

Special thank you to my husband, who always reminds me that I can do anything! He always bets on me!

CONTENTS

PREFACE

If you've picked up this book, you're probably a lot like me: a woman who is inquisitive, ambitious, and driven to do her best. You're capable, willing to work hard, and sitting on a mountain of untapped potential. You've likely experienced a degree of career success, but there have been challenges. And the challenges have left you looking for answers.

How do I get to the next level?
Why doesn't anyone see the value I bring?
What is the right role for me?
How do I move from a job to building a career?
How do I become a better leader?

The answers to your questions reside in you. You are unique, and you have a unique contribution to make to the world. That makes you valuable. The challenge is that we don't always stay grounded in our value because we ignore our authentic voice.

Our inner, authentic voice is that little voice or feeling inside that speaks up when we hit a challenge or a crossroads in our career. I've learned that there are important moments in our careers—Wild Hair moments—when we have the choice to listen to our inner, authentic voice or to ignore it. Each time we dismiss our authentic voice, we step further away from who we are meant to be, further away from our value. When we listen—and act on what we hear—we find answers to the questions that hold us back from realizing our full, authentic potential.

This book is my way of paying forward. It's my way of sharing what I've learned from my experiences and the experiences of other women to help you achieve the career that you deserve. It's full of tips, tools, reflections, and stories to help you find connections, inspiration, and learning.

My hope is that after reading this book, you'll recognize your own Wild Hair moments and listen to your authentic voice to create the career that you love.

CHAPTER 1

MY WILD HAIR MOMENT

As long as we are not ourselves, we will try to be what other people are.

—Malidoma Patrice Somé
Author, *Of Water and the Spirit*

I strode down the hall in my new beige suit and sassy cream blouse. I loved this look! The silk blouse had ruffles in the front and a print of lipstick tubes of different colors against the cream background. I felt feminine and powerful. I was headed to the conference room to meet the leaders of one of our resource groups. Today was our annual meeting with the CEO. I needed to make sure they were prepared.

I entered the conference room, welcomed by hugs and handshakes. As I greeted everyone, I could read nervousness in their body language and their eyes. "We've got a question," one of the co-chairs started. "We were wondering. Should we bring up the discussion of transgender benefits?" I could feel the tension in the air. Our new CEO was an over-60-year-old white man whose most recent role was as CEO of a Catholic health system. Their fight for transgender surgery benefits had been denied numerous times by prior leadership without such a background. They rightfully thought this might be a hot-button topic.

"You must bring up this topic," I said adamantly. "In an inclusive environment, we bring our unique issues and perspectives fully to the table; we don't hold back. That's how problems get solved. This is an important issue. You must speak your truth!" Heads slowly nodded in nervous agreement.

I was giving them the pep talk they needed, but I was preaching to the choir. They could recite these words in their sleep, and so could I. But this time was different. It was all bullshit for me! What I was telling them was 100 percent true. The problem was I wasn't living my truth. I was the chief diversity officer at a Fortune 500 company, and I was hiding something that made me unique—something I had been struggling with for some time: my tightly coiled, wild, African American hair.

I was probably more aware of my "lie" because it was a Monday, right after another "hair weekend." "Hair Weekend" is what I called those weekends when I had a hair appointment that was all-consuming. On Saturday morning, I had gotten up early, just like a workday, to head to the hair salon for the full treatment. It was relaxer Saturday. That meant rising at 7:30 to be in the salon chair by 9:00 for relaxing, washing, conditioning, trimming, drying, flat ironing, and styling.

Relaxing was the most taxing of the processes. I sat in the chair for twenty minutes as my stylist quickly parted my hair into tiny sections and applied the miracle cream, a mix of strong chemicals that break down the cortex of new growth—the unrelaxed hair that had grown in over the last six weeks. Once applied, she'd go back through my hair, section by section, to smooth the cream into the new growth and make sure she covered all of it so that all my natural hair would disappear. Everything would be bone straight, from root to tip. No more wild hair!

The entire process took several hours. After the relaxer application, we headed to the washbowl to rinse out the heavy chemical cream. First, a neutralizing shampoo was used to stop the chemical reaction and remove the sticky cream from my scalp and hair. That was followed by a normal washing and deep conditioning to restore some strength to the hair that I had so mercilessly stripped to straightness. With conditioner still on my hair, it was on to the dryer for fifteen minutes to let the deep conditioning treatment work its magic.

Saturdays were always busy days in the salon, and almost an hour had passed before I sat back down in the stylist chair, hair dripping, for my trim. After a thorough trim, my hair was lathered with creams and lotions and combed into shape for me to head to the dryer again.

After drying and waiting for other clients to rotate out of my stylist's chair, I finally reached her chair again for the styling step. Her skilled hands easily combed through my now straight hair. With a few clips in hand, my stylist sectioned my hair and began the process of flat ironing. Twenty minutes later, she finally began styling my hair in a cute, short bob, my signature style those days.

I looked at myself in the mirror longer than usual that day. "When will you have the nerve to stop this never-ending cycle of relax, color, cut, repeat?" I thought to myself. I couldn't. The stakes were just too high. I was different, and I knew it because I saw the difference each day.

Difference in the Workplace

I worked in human resources, where you get to see and hear a lot about how leaders and others think about people. There are continual conversations about the talent (i.e., the people) in the company. When there are new projects or new leadership opportunities, talent is discussed. If a department is going to be restructured, talent is discussed. On a regular cycle of planning for succession, talent is discussed. Talent is a primary, daily focus for human resources, as it should be.

I had the opportunity to participate in many conversations about talent. I heard the comments about everything that was right about some individuals. I heard the comments about developmental needs and opportunities for other individuals. I heard the comments about talented individuals who just didn't quite fit the role they held or had something missing that was intangible and couldn't be described.

I could see that often, the fact that an individual was male and white slanted the conversations in their favor, even for those who may have been struggling in their roles. It became clear to me that it was risky to be a Black woman striving to high levels of leadership if you didn't look the part. The last thing I wanted to do was to put another check in the column of difference. The more my hair looked like the majority (i.e., relaxed and straight), the better. I had to continue that cycle of relax, color, cut. I had to minimize my difference.

A few months later, I took a girls' trip with my best friend, her sister, and her daughter. We headed to Jamaica for some serious downtime. In preparation, I got my hair braided into a beautiful style with goddess braids. For four days, I woke late each morning and walked a few miles on the beach with my braids twisted atop my head, the sun warming my skin, and the breeze lovingly caressing me. No curling irons or hair sprays made the trip! The days were unscripted, unencumbered, authentic. We were ourselves in our purest forms.

When I returned home and removed the braids, I had an opportunity. I had allowed my relaxed hair to grow out for several weeks prior to the trip. Since the trip, my hair had grown even more. I had a couple of inches of natural hair! Do I follow my heart and stay natural, or do I return to the comfort and safety of relaxed hair? I already had a hair appointment scheduled, so I'd be ready to head back to work on Monday. I felt the excitement of opportunity mixed with the pang of change churning in my stomach when I thought about this.

Natural hair was foreign to me. I had been relaxing my hair since I was 12 years old. Everything I learned growing up said to relax my hair because natural hair wasn't good hair. It was wild hair! It wasn't easy to comb or deal with if it wasn't relaxed. It was a problem!

Everything I'd learned in the corporate world said straight, relaxed hair was best. There were very few Black executives where I worked, and none of the women wore natural hairstyles. How could I return to work with my natural hair? What signal would that send to people in human resources and other leaders who would be making decisions about my career? What would be said about me when my abilities were discussed? Would I be one of the ones who "just didn't fit"?

In my role, I relied heavily on my influence to get things done. Would I be perceived as less credible, less influential if I no longer looked like the executives around me? What should I do? I decided I would make the call when I sat in my stylist's chair that next day.

I drove to the hair salon, determined not to think about what I would do. It was just too hard to imagine keeping my hair natural. I couldn't imagine being able to take care of it. I couldn't imagine how the people at work would react. I just couldn't imagine my world with me having natural hair. I couldn't see myself. And what you can't see, you can't be. Right?

I sat in the stylist's chair, my mind made up, as she draped the cape over me and asked about my trip to Jamaica. I started to share the details of the trip as she organized her counter and prepared to relax my hair. I stopped talking. I got a wild hair. "I want to go natural!" I blurted out before I could stop myself.

Wearing a natural style herself, my stylist squealed with delight. "You are going to love it!" At that moment, I felt a huge release of stress. I was no longer afraid. I felt free. I had spoken my truth. I felt more like me than I had ever felt in the past. I wasn't sure what my first day back to work would be like, but I believed that whatever happened, I could handle it because I was living my truth. The moment had presented itself, and I had chosen my authenticity.

Back at work, people were shocked. I received compliments and open-mouthed gasps as people searched for words. My assistant said my new style made me look younger! One of my colleagues, a Black woman with relaxed hair, commented, jokingly, that I was "taking this diversity thing seriously!" "I'm just doing me," I responded. I felt a tingle of strength run through me.

Over the years, as I have continued to let my natural hair grow and become an even greater part of my style, so many women, especially Black women, have asked me how I did it. As I've talked with them, I've learned that they really want to know how I managed to be true to myself, garner the respect of my colleagues, and be influential and successful at work. They want to know: How have I managed to create an authentic, successful career?

When I reflected on this question, I realized that while my hair decision might have been my most visible moment, I've navigated many Wild Hair moments throughout my career, and I bet you have too. In each of these moments, making the authentic choice helped me transform and create the career that I loved. I didn't always get it right; I didn't always make the authentic choice. Sometimes I didn't even realize that there was an authentic choice to be made. Other times it took a couple of tries before I listened to my authentic voice and followed its lead.

Creating an Authentic Career

What does it mean to create an authentic career? How is creating an authentic career different from simply creating a career? It all starts with perspective.

Creating an authentic career is all about viewing yourself and your career choices through a multi-dimensional lens of honesty, courage, confidence, and resilience. Self-honesty is a priority. This means being honest with yourself about what you want or need or feel. It means being honest with yourself about what you are or are not doing and how well or poorly you are doing it. Honesty creates accountability within yourself and charts the course for the authentic career you can create. Your authentic career starts with honesty.

When we look at ourselves and our careers through the lens of courage, we ask ourselves what we fear most and what we would do if we were not afraid. We see career challenges truly as opportunities to rise to a new level of performance and to set new standards and goals for ourselves. We are willing to be uncomfortable for the sake of growing more toward who we are meant to be. We confront hard choices head-on with the belief that we will succeed.

We create authentic careers when we have a true appreciation of our gifts, talents, skills, experiences, knowledge, and all the things that make us unique—including our wild hair! This appreciation creates confidence in ourselves and our capabilities. Making confident career choices and decisions is how we demonstrate appreciation for and trust in ourselves.

We create authentic careers when we embrace trust and believe that we will thrive because of our career choices or survive despite them. Resilience comes from trusting that our authentic self uniquely prepares us for all that we seek in our careers. That, in fact, our authentic, unique selves can create our future career opportunities if we listen and follow our authentic voices. We embrace resilience when we are not afraid of having to bounce back or recreate or recover from a career decision. We know that we are tough, pliable, and complete.

When something is out of sync with your authenticity (i.e., a decision challenges your honesty, courage, confidence, or resilience), you will feel or hear your authentic voice guiding you to make the decision that is best for you. Sometimes we ignore our authentic voice because the choice is not easy or comfortable. Sometimes we resist our authentic feelings because we will be different if we make our authentic choice. Sometimes we worry about how we will be viewed, perceived, or treated if we make the authentic choice. Sometimes we worry about making others uncomfortable. Making authentic career choices is not about ignoring your environment. It's about finding a way to bring your full self into your environment for the better. It's about being true to yourself.

Over the years of my career, there were many tough Wild Hair moments. Each time I made my authentic choice, I became increasingly clear about my value at work and the difference I made. My impact grew, and success followed. I passed my lessons on to other women who grew their authenticity, impact, and success one authentic moment at a time. Instead of dividing our attention and energy between who we were and who we wanted to be, our energy went toward creating a career that we loved, moment by moment, choice by choice.

Are you ready to create an authentic career that you love? No one can be a better you than you! Let's get started.

Authenticity Lessons & Reflections

1. **Self-honesty creates the path to an authentic career.** Examine your career through the lens of self-honesty. *How do you feel about your career? How has your career met your expectations? How has your career failed to meet your expectations? What has been the greatest challenge to creating an authentic career that you love?*

2. **Courage is not the absence of fear. Courage is fear in action.** *What fear stops you from moving forward in your career? What would you need to move forward with courage?*

3. **Confidence starts with self-appreciation.** Take time to appreciate the skills, talents, experiences, and qualities that make you unique. *What do you appreciate most about yourself? How could your career be different if you built it around the capabilities you appreciate most?*

4. **Trust what makes you unique, powerful, and resilient.** Find strength in the skill, talent, or quality that makes you uniquely you. Use it to establish your brand or platform to drive change. *What skill, talent, or quality best defines you? How can you use that skill, talent, or quality to impact your work or advance your career?*

5. **Embrace your Wild Hair moments by listening to your authentic voice.** *When have you experienced a Wild Hair moment? What did your authentic voice tell you, and how did you use what you heard?*

CHAPTER 2

DO YOU SEE WHAT OTHERS SEE?

Authentic success requires honesty. You need to know yourself—your capabilities, challenges, likes, and dislikes. But it's not easy to be absolutely and totally honest with ourselves. We all have blind spots.

When we're building a career, it helps to have an honest, outside perspective to help you develop and grow. Some look to mentors for that perspective. But you need more than a mentor; you need a truth-teller to create authentic success.

Truth-Tellers: Authentic Mentorship

What is a truth-teller? A truth-teller is more than a mentor. Mentorship is about long-term career and personal development. A mentor offers advice, guidance, and support to the mentee.

A truth-teller does everything a mentor does, and they know you well enough to raise the bar when you're flying too low and pull your reigns when you're moving too fast.

Truth-tellers are guided by your goals, but they don't let your goals blind them to your career truth. They are experienced and willing to share. They are committed to your growth and development, and they are honest at all costs.

Truth-tellers live in their own authenticity, and they share their authentic knowledge and experience with everyone they mentor. Through their honesty, truth-tellers compel action. Truth-tellers are catalysts that can jumpstart or energize a career. Truth-tellers have an edge: they are mentors who won't be satisfied until you get the most out of your career. They can't stand for you to be any less than you are capable of being, and they won't set you up for failure by pushing you to do more than you're ready to do. There's no slacking or faking it with a truth-teller.

My Truth-Teller

I began my career as an entry-level claims processor for a local health insurance company. I'll never forget my hire date: 8/8/88. After a twelve-week training class, I was officially on my own and processing claims for northern Ohio.

By the early 1990s, my company, like other health insurers, wanted to take a giant leap forward with technology and automation. The company pulled together a group of employees who left their regular roles to join a project called the Managed Care Acceleration Project, or MCAP. This project was run by a dynamic female leader. She was responsible for the project as well as the centralized claims unit, which relied heavily on automation to streamline processes and improve productivity.

Now a business analyst, I was tapped to join the MCAP team in its infancy. IBM was our external partner helping to guide us through the journey of fundamentally rethinking and reengineering our core operational processes. My first role was as a team member on several of the project work teams. A few months in, I was assigned to lead the provider team. It was my first management role! I had two project managers reporting directly to me.

All aspects of operations were under a microscope. We were redefining the underlying models for how processes and systems work to operationalize health insurance. Part of accomplishing such a herculean task was building out the right team to move work forward.

Several months into the project, our leader decided on the structure needed to best execute these new processes. She defined several critical senior leadership roles that were to be filled. These roles were highly sought after. They were leadership roles on the most important project in the company at the time. The visibility across the company and exposure to executive management could help accelerate your career.

Everyone was talking about the new job opportunities and which ones they were most interested in and planning to apply for. I was a mere spectator to it all. I was in my first management role, and I thought that was enough for me. I had my own struggles figuring out how to keep people on my team motivated while addressing daily project questions and decisions, completing timecards, etc.

I was too new to my role to even think about a bigger position, and I was sure that our leader was thinking about me the same way. It would have been mighty bold of me to think I could compete with my peers, many of whom had years of management experience and held roles higher than mine. The time simply wasn't right.

One of my peers on the project was an African American woman who I respected greatly. I'll call her Ms. M. She was a mentor to me because she was always willing to pull me aside and share insights and teach me. It was early in my management career, and I didn't have an aptitude or appetite for work politics.

Ms. M had an uncanny ability to see and anticipate underlying politics related to almost any issue or decision. Her political savvy was an example of her abilities to analyze people and situations thoroughly. One of the most valuable things she taught me was to understand the value that people bring to any situation, the role they play, and the contribution that they make in different circumstances. Ms. M was masterful at understanding her value and contribution and building teams around her that helped complement her weaknesses while building collective synergy. She was awesome!

One day, while all the whispering and speculation about the open positions was at its height, Ms. M asked me to join her at the library so we could get away from the office and work on our project plans without interruption. I quickly agreed because I always loved spending time with her. She was a goldmine to me. I loved her!

We made our way to University of Cincinnati Library and unpacked our things in one of the study rooms. We were just settling into our respective work when Ms. M said, "Now you know I didn't bring you here to work on our projects, right?" I was stunned. What were we here for? She continued, "I brought you here because I want to talk to you about those open jobs. Have you applied for any of them?"

I told her I had not applied for any of the positions, and she wanted to know why not. I explained, "I don't think those jobs are for me. I'm new to management. I barely know what I'm doing as I manage my current team. Those leadership roles are for you and the others with way more experience. Plus, I don't even think anyone thinks I could do one of those jobs. I'm too new. The timing isn't right."

Ms. M began to lift me up like only a caring mentor can do. She saw in me what I didn't see for myself. She explained to me that I was more than smart enough for one of those roles. She shared that she would be there to support me whenever I needed it. And that I shouldn't count myself out without first throwing my hat in the ring!

I sat there, shocked. There was so much to take in. I told her I would think it over. She told me not to think too long! The interview and selection process would be kicking off soon. I needed to decide and act if I was going to do it. And if I wasn't going to act, that was a decision too. I needed to be OK with that decision and not have regrets.

After talking it over with my husband, Anthony, I decided that it couldn't hurt to apply. There were three open positions. Two of the roles reported to the third, and the third reported to the senior executive leader. All were at least two levels above the position I held.

The process was being facilitated by HR with an external recruitment partner as there was a battery of psychological and intellectual tests and interviews to complete in addition to traditional interviews. I was nervous as I went through the process. I repeatedly reminded myself that I had nothing to lose. I had not even thought about these roles as available to me. The timing wasn't right. Right? Any outcome would be OK. Right? Even if I didn't get one of the positions, I was getting great exposure through the process. HR and senior leadership would know that I wanted to grow in my career. Right?

The big day came when I was called to the executive vice president's office to discuss the roles. I was so nervous. Why? I had nothing to lose, right? She was a tall, imposing woman who had a crass sense of humor and could be very direct. I liked her. She sat down across from me and asked me what I thought about the process and how I thought I did. I told her I did my best and that I had enjoyed the process, which was true.

I guessed that the small talk was leading up to "thank you for your interest, but we decided to go with someone who has more experience." She shared with me that I had performed the best throughout the process. My heart leaped! But that she was not going to give me the top job, reporting to her. My heart sank!

She went on to explain that while I had the intellect, talent, and skills, I didn't have the lived experience needed to be successful in that job. I had not managed managers. I had not dealt with highly political and sensitive issues with other senior leaders. "Those guys would eat you alive!" she said as she slammed her hand on the table for emphasis.

She believed that I would get to a senior leadership role one day, but I needed to pace myself. She placed me in the director role for the claims unit. I would report to the person who would report directly to her. I went from managing two employees to leading an organization of over 75 employees—almost overnight.

I walked out of the office, trying to contain my smile. I had mixed emotions: fear of the new, big job I had received, pride in my performance during the selection process, hurt from being told I was not ready for more, and gratitude. I was grateful for my mentor, who saw my capabilities. I was grateful for my leader, who saw my limitations. These were two wise women who learned from their own experiences and chose to pass their knowledge on to me. They were truth-tellers. They pushed and pulled me along at just the right pace.

Finding the Right Truth-Teller

Sometimes we organically find truth-tellers: our career path intersects with someone, like Ms. M, and we form a relationship. Or, if we're lucky, our boss takes on the role.

Some relationships are formal, such as formal mentorship programs that are often included in high-potential development programs. Some are informal. Some are long-lasting relationships, and others are short term. No matter how the relationship comes to be, the goal is for the relationship to be grounded in honesty and focused on helping you to be your best, doing your best work at what you want to do.

You want to create a career that is based on your authentic self, one where your unique skills, talents, and experiences are the drivers. To do that well, you must have truth-tellers helping you along the way.

Be intentional about the mentors in your life and ensure you include truth-tellers by looking for a few key attributes:

Mutual Respect: Be sure that you respect your truth-teller. Respect their work, their skills, their leadership, everything. And be sure they respect you and the journey you are on.

Mutual Honesty: Your truth-teller must be willing and able to be honest and direct with you. And you must be able to do the same. Let your potential truth-teller know that you want their honest assessment of your skills, talent, and experience, and be honest about your goals.

Experience/Expertise: Make sure your truth-teller has experience or expertise that aligns with your needs. This can be as broad as holding a leadership position or as specific as cost accounting experience.

Commitment to Your Success: The key distinction that elevates mentorship to truth-telling is the commitment to your success.

Truth-tellers commit their time, their expertise, and their energy toward igniting your potential. They raise the bar, and they challenge you. They are all about how to make you better. It's not about how much time they spend with you—it's about the intentionality of that time and the wisdom that is imparted. They are a partner in your journey, whether they are by your side through a one-hour session or a lifetime relationship. You feel their commitment.

And remember, when you're in a mentoring relationship, the mentee does the work. That's you! You must act on the insights you glean from your truth-teller to create the authentic career that you love.

Authenticity in Action

As chief diversity officer, I often spoke about career management at town halls and team meetings. It was not uncommon for women who wanted career guidance to reach out to me after hearing me speak. After one such speech to an operations team, a young woman contacted me for coaching.

"I've been with the company for a couple of years. I absolutely love it here, but I want to grow. I know that I can do more than my job right now," she explained. She was early in her career and great at her job. People in the department came to her with their questions because of her deep knowledge, and she was often asked to lend her expertise on projects.

But she couldn't seem to get a project management lead role. In a frustrated voice, the young woman explained, "I've told my manager that I want to grow and to be a project manager. She agreed to give me more opportunities to be on project teams. I don't just want to be on the teams. I want to lead the teams! It's like my manager doesn't hear me or doesn't care. I guess I'll just have to go to another company where I can have a career."

Instead of focusing on what others weren't doing for her, I asked, "What are you doing to become a project manager?" She was quiet. I asked her if she knew the responsibilities of a project manager in-depth and if she was prepared to take on a project manager role? Her sheepish, incomplete response told me everything.

She needed someone to do more than pacify her with the offer to serve on another team. She needed a truth-teller who could help her understand project management and identify potential areas in the organization that might be best suited for her career growth. She needed someone who could honestly give her feedback on her skills and goals and had the experience and knowledge of the organization to help point her in the right direction.

We talked about the qualities of a good truth-teller and some potential women and men who might work. Her homework was to reach out to those individuals, schedule a time to introduce herself, discuss her goals, and ask for authentic mentorship. We would have another call in a month to see how things were going.

Asking for authentic mentorship is not always easy. Most people fear reaching out to someone they don't know personally, especially if the individual is in a much higher position. It also can be a challenge to ask someone you've just met to give you honest feedback.

In our one-month check-in meeting, the young woman explained, "I put off reaching out for as long as I could, but I knew we were meeting, so I finally sent the emails last week. I couldn't believe it when I got a response back the same day from one of the leaders I contacted! We've scheduled a meeting. I couldn't believe that she would make time for me!"

In my career, I've found that most people are willing to share their knowledge and be a mentor. But all mentors are not created equal; so, don't settle! Be sure to find a truth-teller, someone who will take the time to get to know you and offer honest, authentic guidance, not just share their own career story.

In our third and last coaching session, the young woman shared a little about her first conversation with her truth-teller. This leader was outside of her department and had responsibility for project managers, an obvious great choice to assess project management skills. "My mentor told me what it takes to be a project manager. She said I have the potential, but I've got some work to do," she explained with excitement. "I'm going to start by taking some project management courses and ask my manager if I can lead a small project for our team. I've got some ideas on things that could be improved in the department, and I think my manager will let me take the lead." The leader had helped this woman identify her strengths and opportunities and encouraged her to develop her skills in pursuit of her career goals. Having the support of an authentic mentor, i.e., truth-teller, moved her to action. She found her Ms. M!

It's easier to act when we're honest about what we want and where we stand. Ask yourself:

- *What is my career goal?*
- *What unique skills, experiences, talents, and knowledge will help me achieve my goal?*
- *What am I doing to make my goal a reality?*

When we pivot our thinking from placing ownership on others (e.g., "my manager doesn't hear me") to honest ownership of our career goals (e.g., "what are you doing to become a project manager"), we move to action. With the help of a truth-teller, you get the honesty you need to keep fueling the action engine.

Authenticity Lessons & Reflections

1. **Don't doubt yourself. Know yourself.** Be honest with yourself about your education, skills, experience, talents, potential, and goals. Don't wait for an opportunity to become available to be thoughtful about your capabilities. *What are your strengths? What are your limitations? What opportunities have you consciously (or subconsciously) ignored or missed? What changes in skills, experience, talent, or education do you need to make to be ready for the next opportunity?*

2. **Get a truth-teller in your life.** Identify mentors or others you can trust who will tell you the truth about your capabilities. *Who are your mentors and truth-tellers? What insight do you need most from them to advance your career?*

3. **Just because you think it doesn't mean it's true.** Don't allow limiting thoughts to stifle your potential. Don't be afraid to dream big, then work hard to make it happen. Get a coach to hold you accountable. *What are your limiting thoughts? How can you validate reality? What is your big dream? What do you need to do to make it happen?*

CHAPTER 3

THE SHADOW OF AN UNEXPECTED LEADER

Are leaders born or made? Before I had my first leadership role, I would have responded "born" because I had been a leader throughout my early years. I was the oldest child, and my parents always looked to me to take the lead, make the right decisions, and look out for my siblings.

I was in ballet as a child and played the lead role in our recitals. I was head of the student council in high school, captain of the volleyball team, and head of the Black Cultural Workshop. I was a born leader, or so I thought until I was in my first real leadership position at work. It was then that I realized that I had been asking the wrong question. I should have asked myself: How can I be an authentic leader? I quickly learned that anyone can be placed in a leadership role, but not all leaders are authentic.

What is Authentic Leadership?

Before I dive into authentic leadership, let's talk about the leadership shadow. I first learned about the leadership shadow while participating in training in culture shaping provided by the Senn Delaney organization.[1] The concept is simple: as a leader, you have a shadow that you cast across the organization. This shadow gives employees cues about the culture of the organization, i.e., what it's like to work there, as well as the norms, habits, and behaviors that are expected for success.

Your leadership shadow is driven by your state of mind, your mood, and how you show up each day at work. To take that concept a little further, the leadership shadow also provides people with a perspective on you as a leader. The challenge for us is creating a shadow that authentically represents who we are as a leader versus what either we, our organizations, or others expect us to be.

Sometimes, as leaders, we become torn between the shadow we are expected to project and our true selves. How do we reconcile who we are with the leader we want to be and cast an authentic leadership shadow?

The truth is leadership often doesn't feel natural, much less authentic. Stepping into a leadership role for the first time or moving into a new leadership role can feel like putting on a new pair of pumps—you look good, but you're slightly uncomfortable!

Sometimes it's because we're new to the role and uncomfortable as we're learning. Other times—especially as women and women of

---

[1] Larry Senn, Jim Hart, and 2020, "What Leadership Shadow Do You Cast?" Shadow of the leader (Heidrick & Struggles, June 23, 2015), https://www.heidrick.com/Knowledge-Center/Article/What-leadership-shadow-do-you-cast.

color—it's because we can't reconcile what we see and experience as leadership with both our beliefs about what good leadership looks like and our beliefs about ourselves.

We've seen women in our lives lead—our mothers, grandmothers, sisters, and aunts. But women leaders can be in short supply in the corporate world. When the leaders around us don't look like us, we don't receive the unspoken feedback and validation that who we are is more than enough to lead well. That can shake your confidence and make you question how you will lead in a way that feels honest and true to you. Without role models to provide the unspoken reinforcement that you can be successful as a woman, it's easy to question yourself and to feel alone in your leadership. Because of these factors, for women, leading authentically requires courage.

Leading authentically means there is a strong connection between who you are and how you lead. It means the leadership shadow you cast looks like you and no one else. Your leadership does not feel like a betrayal of who you are. It doesn't feel artificial. It doesn't feel like you're hiding something about yourself. There's no dissonance between you and your leadership.

Dissonance occurs when there is a disconnect between who you are and how you present yourself as a leader. It creates stress because you spend so much energy being the leader that you think you should be versus being the true leader that you're capable of being. When dissonance enters the equation, our leadership shadow becomes a cold, barren place for our followers to live under and not a place of warmth and growth.

When you lead authentically, you bring the best of you and what makes you unique into your leadership. If you have a strong sense of humor, it's a part of your leadership. If you are reflective and introverted, it's a part of your leadership. If you're analytical, it's a part of your leadership. When others interact with you as a leader, they know who you are and what you stand for.

Learning to Be a Leader

When I got my first big leadership role, I had no idea what it meant to be a leader. The last couple of months before my promotion to director of the claims unit, I had been a manager of two people. In my new leadership position, I was managing a unit of seventy-five employees. I was now a manager of managers. I had so much to learn. Nonetheless, I was excited! I felt that I had truly arrived in the ranks of leadership.

I was an unexpected choice for my new role. While I had been a business analyst for a few years, including supporting the needs of the claims department, I was an unknown to the managers and employees in the department. Their previous leader was very well known. She had a strong reputation for getting things done—her way. She had worked with many of the team for a long time and had truly put the department on the map as a group leading the way in automation and innovation. The managers were fiercely loyal to her. Knowing all of this, I was humbled to be in the position and felt my primary focus coming into the new role would be to learn and determine how I could contribute to their continued success.

I updated my wardrobe to look the part. I was confident as I walked straight down the long aisle through the middle of the department to get to my office the first morning. I kept moving at a steady clip, with intention, to my office. After all, I rationalized, leaders were always busy and on the go to the next meeting or call or something. I stayed in my office that day, checking email and reading information. Except for lunch, I only emerged to leave for the evening, when almost everyone was gone for the day. I kept that routine going, and the first couple of weeks went by quickly.

About three weeks into my new role, I heard a knock at my door one morning. I ushered one of my managers in and offered her a seat as I went back to my big chair behind my desk. (That's where leaders are supposed to sit. Right?) She looked a little nervous as she shared that she had been nominated to come to talk with me. Nominated? OK, where is this going?

"Is everything OK?" she asked.

"Yes, I'm great. Why do you ask?" I responded. Boy, the hospitality was unbelievable. They were concerned about me!

The manager went on, "Is everything OK with the company right now? Is our department OK? Are we doing a good job?"

I interrupted her questioning and asked, "What's going on?" She explained that because I came in every day and went straight to my office without speaking to anyone, the team was worried that something was either wrong with me or that they had somehow not been performing. We were having meetings as a management team, but I wasn't sharing anything that connected them to the rest of the company. I didn't engage with the team. The department had been so visible and talked about before I came, and now, they felt like they didn't exist, and nobody cared about their work.

Wow! I felt the air leave my body and thought to myself, "Don't cry!" I thought I was working hard and doing good work, only to find out that my managers thought I was letting the department down. They felt like the department no longer mattered to the company. I had been entrusted with the leadership of this department, and in three short weeks, I had lowered the confidence of the management team. By behaving the way I thought a leader should (rather than as the leader I was), I had cast a dark, ugly, cold leadership shadow!

I listened intently to the feedback, fighting back my tears. "The team needs to hear from you," the manager said. Before she left my office, we agreed that I would hold a department meeting before the end of the week. I had no idea what I would say to everyone in that meeting, but it felt like the right next step.

Embarrassed by the pep talk I'd been given, I was despondent yet determined to figure out how I could do better. I spent the evening replaying the conversation with the brave manager. She was right. I was supporting but not leading.

What did it mean to lead? I guessed it meant that I needed to start communicating more about the performance of our unit and the overall organization. This didn't come naturally to me. I knew I was an introvert. I liked to think things through and analyze. I operated at my best when I operated alone. I didn't need many friends or many personal interactions to be content.

If leading the department meant constant interactions, big unit meetings, and sharing my thoughts about our performance and the organization, how could I ever be happy in a leadership role? How could I still be myself and lead this department?

I continued to reflect (as introverts do). How would I reconcile my introversion with my leadership responsibilities? How could I be true to myself while serving others? How could I create a leadership shadow I was proud of and one that reflected who I really was as a person? I would need to change my approach to my role, my behaviors, and my actions. Was I capable of this?

The day of the meeting, the entire unit of 75 employees gathered in an open area. It was a little overwhelming. I felt my legs shaking beneath me as I nervously began telling my audience about myself, "I'll never forget my first day: 8/8/88. Kind of like 666 in *The Omen*!"

That generated a few nervous laughs, so I relaxed, and the discussion began to flow effortlessly.

I drew on one of my strengths—humility. I shared that my role was new to me, and I was still learning. But I was also excited and committed. I talked about how the department was performing and shared updates about the organization. The team asked questions, and I answered to the best of my ability. The energy level was high, and people were engaged and excited, and so was I.

How to Be an Authentic Leader

As the story above shows, being a leader requires effort. Being an authentic female leader requires effort and courage. I've found that it helps to use the following tips as a guide.

Know what it means to lead, especially at your organization. Each organization is different, but one thing is consistent: when you become a leader, you give up "me" for the collective "we." "We" means the team you lead, the team you are a part of, and the collective team—the organization. The days of "I" and "me" are gone. A leader agrees to take responsibility for the outcomes from the efforts of the team they lead, the collective results of the team they are part of, and for achieving the goals of the overall organization.

Delivering on these responsibilities requires skill in a variety of areas: communication, collaboration, decision-making, strategy, talent development, performance management, goal setting, execution, and many more. You can research these topics and attend seminars and conferences to get the basics, but it is most important to understand how these skills show up in your organization. For example, what decisions do you control as a leader? What are you expected to collaborate on versus handle independently? Is communication primarily written or verbal? When is verbal communication used?

Analyzing the organization's leadership style gives insight into what is expected of you as a leader. Knowing this will help you determine if your values and style are a fit with the values of the organization and how those values are expressed in the leadership expectations. If you are aligned with the values and expectations of leaders at the organization, then it's worth bringing your unique leadership to the team. Not all organizations are worthy of your authenticity.

Have a growth mindset. Being a leader is work. You won't be perfect at everything. When you go into a leadership role, assess your skill set against what is expected, and ask for feedback. Get a truth-teller to mentor you on leadership. Address gaps, and don't give up if the new skills feel uncomfortable. Find ways to execute your new skills with your brand of authentic leadership. Working through the discomfort to acquire new skills and make them your own expands your authenticity.

Bring your uniqueness to the table. Leadership requires creativity and problem-solving. Problems are best solved when unique perspectives are brought to the solutions table. Staying quiet or disengaged when you have a point of view or an idea dishonors you, and it makes any group you're working with less effective.

Be honest, caring, and forthright. Most days, it will be easy to lead with integrity. But sometimes you will be challenged. Many times, as a leader, you will have knowledge and information that cannot be shared with everyone, especially the people you have the privilege to lead. You must have integrity while being honest, caring, and forthright. Finding your way to share what you can is critical. Sometimes you may not have an answer for the question or challenge presented to you. Taking ownership for finding the answer is what's most important.

When you are honest, caring, and forthright, you show respect for the people who work for you and with you. And you respect yourself by leading with authentic integrity.

Own being a leader—always. There is a distinction between being the leader or being among those who are led. Some leaders straddle the line between those they lead and stepping fully into leadership. When the tough decisions are to be shared, leaders who are straddling will place ownership of the decision anywhere but on themselves—thus placing themselves among the led—when they are really a part of the collective leadership of the organization. There is no part-time leader. You either are a leader or you are among the led. Stay grounded in your leadership, even when it's difficult. You may feel vulnerable to people disliking you or your decisions, but vulnerability is key to authenticity. You are being true to yourself as a leader.

Tell your leadership story. Know your story of why and how you became a leader and tell that story often, especially to other women. Your story empowers others, but more importantly, it will give you strength when you need it. It will remind you of where you started and how you've developed your authentic leadership style. Your story will remind you that you are authentically capable and enough.

Authenticity in Action

When we think about our leadership shadow, sometimes we may think about ourselves very narrowly and only consider our "work selves." Your best leadership will come from accessing all the skills and attributes at your disposal, even the ones you may think have no place at work. I coached a woman, Ms. A, who was recently promoted to a senior leader role, leading her former peers, a large team of analysts. A stellar analyst, known for her ability to translate complex analytics into simple-speak for customers, this leader was working to define her style as a leader to her new and former peers.

Her style as an analyst had been direct and analytical. Now, as a leader, that style was not working well. She struggled with motivating her team under enormous staffing constraints and conveying to her peers the challenges in meeting their expectations.

In one of our coaching conversations, she confessed, "This is hard. I just want to tell my whole team to buck up and get over it. We're not getting any additional staff anytime soon, and leadership expects us to get this done yesterday. But I don't want to be known as a bitch. I want to show them support. I care about these people, and I know how hard their work is right now. What do I do? I feel like I'm failing."

My response was, "Who do you want to be as a leader? The one who says, 'buck up' or the one who cares, demonstrates support, and gets work done?"

Outside of work, she was nurturing. She was actively involved in her children's school lives and volunteered in her community. Her heart was huge, but she was stifling that huge heart at work for fear of being perceived as soft and ineffective. But carrying the corporate message of "no resources" with a tough "buck up" tone was going to cast a leadership shadow that wasn't consistent with the nurturing, supportive leader she wanted to be.

Over the next several coaching sessions, we worked through a model that enabled her to establish a comfortable leadership brand that was uniquely her own. She believed in the values of the company, i.e., becoming more efficient, doing work that aligned with strategy. Her challenge was working through the discomfort of reconciling her corporate message as a leader with a communication style and approach that was authentically hers.

In one of our last sessions, she discussed how she was handling restructuring her team and the difficult decisions she was making to best align resources and be effective. Her first approach was a team meeting that had not gone as well as planned, but she didn't give up. She explained, "I think our meeting was okay, and most of the team are on board. But I still have a few people who don't seem to understand that things need to change. They're important members of my leadership team, so I'm going to meet with them one-on-one to discuss how these changes impact each of them individually."

She took the difficult messages to her team leaders individually, acknowledging that her changes weren't going to be easy. She received negative and challenging feedback from some of them, but she stayed consistent in her supportive yet direct approach.

When we debriefed after her individual meetings, she shared, "I'm exhausted, but I feel like I'm finally establishing myself with my team. They didn't like everything I had to say, but they seemed to understand. I think they respect me as their leader now. I can live with that! Plus, my boss says he can see the difference I'm making, and that's a success." Once she tapped into the nurturing and supportive style that she exhibited in her personal life, Ms. A became a more effective leader and cast a leadership shadow that made her proud.

Being a successful, authentic leader takes courage. You must be willing to leave your comfort zone to grow into the leader YOU want to be—not what you think a leader should be or what other leaders look like at your company. Leaving your comfort zone doesn't mean you're untrue to yourself. It simply means you're expanding the definition of your authenticity. When you lead authentically, there's no energy lost on navigating between who you are and the leadership role you play. Your leadership shadow reflects who you are. Your potential and impact are magnified.

Authenticity Lessons & Reflections

1. **Leadership is demanding and requires courage. Your role is not to do but to lead.** Understand that going into your role, and work to develop and refine your leadership skills. *How is your leadership role different from your last role? What new or unexpected activities or responsibilities do you now have? What skills do you need to develop or refine?*

2. **Know the leadership shadow you cast.** How you present yourself and engage with others every day creates your personal leadership shadow. Focus on the experience you want to create for those that work for you and with you. *How do you present yourself at work? How are you engaging with your direct team, peers, leadership? How well does your leadership shadow (i.e., how others experience you) reflect your authentic self? What could you change to cast the shadow you'd be proud of?*

3. **Reconcile who you are with your leadership role to expand your authenticity.** If your values align with the expectations of your new role, step outside your comfort zone to learn new skills and behaviors. If your values don't align with those expectations, consider finding a new role. *What are your values? What activities at work are taking you outside your comfort zone? How can you reconcile those activities with your values?*

CHAPTER 4

CRUCIBLE MOMENTS

Crucible \ˈkro͞osəb(ə)l
A situation of severe trial, or in which different elements interact, leading to the creation of something new.

—*New Oxford American Dictionary*

Mother, wife, sister, daughter, best friend, vice president, chief diversity officer, board member, boss, employee, volunteer, mentor, coach, confidante. Just when I was about to fit another hat on my head, someone kindly advised me that I needed more "work-life balance." Funny!

It's impossible to balance work and life because, for most of us, work is a part of life, not something separate that we can adjust on the fly to make the scales even out. To build an authentic career, it's not about balance or integration. It's not even about work. It's about you, your values, and alignment between the two. Sometimes it takes a crucible moment to clarify your values and create that alignment.

Authentic Values Alignment

Women struggle with work-life balance in a way that is vastly different from men. Because society has traditionally defined men as the working breadwinner of the household, when a woman works, many view this as an additional responsibility that must not replace or outweigh her other responsibilities as a woman, such as being a wife or mother.

In fact, many women struggle with a mentality that they must do all things well (remain highly engaged at work, active in the PTA, plan weekly date nights with their partners, etc.). They feel pressure to juggle it all and do it all well.

Other women make sure they separate work from home so that they are not viewed, especially by men, as being distracted by motherhood or other responsibilities outside of work. They double down on work and make themselves available at all costs.

Then there are others, like me, who love their families and also love the challenge, the sense of accomplishment, and the fulfillment that working brings. The bigger the challenge, the harder we work.

No matter how we get there, we all arrive at the same impasse: work takes over. Work-life balance isn't the solution. Authentic values alignment is the solution.

Authentic values alignment simply means we know what we value, we know where work aligns with those values (i.e., our priorities), and we live authentically to that alignment. The challenge is that we are rarely prepared for the crucible moment that happens when things are out of alignment.

My Crucible Moment

I was thirty years old when I gave birth to my first child. I finished my bachelor's degree in accounting in December 1995. My husband, Anthony, and I purchased our first house in September 1996, and on July 1 of the next year, Devan, our first daughter, was born. Devan was a bright light after three years of challenging times.

I took a full twelve weeks of maternity leave. I spent my time learning my new role as a mother, relying heavily on my own mom for advice. One night, after trying everything, we could not get Devan to sleep. She just cried constantly. Anthony and I had tried everything, to no avail. After a call to my mom at 3 a.m., I was reassured that nothing was wrong with our daughter, and I calmed myself enough to rock her to sleep. My mom was my best friend. I relied on her for so many things, and she always came through for me.

Summertime meant budget cycle at work. Despite being on leave, since it was my first time establishing a budget for my new organization, I worked on my budget in between nursing and naps. I also addressed a couple of HR issues that had come up. The twelve weeks went by quickly, and I headed back to work in the middle of September.

In the early days of being back at work, it was difficult to find the focus I needed. I just wanted to work and get back to my child, who was being cared for by my mother. After the first week, I started to notice that my mom seemed to be out of energy when I got to her house. She was lethargic, and her eyes were jaundiced. We scheduled a doctor's appointment for the Friday morning of my second week back to work.

On the morning of the doctor's appointment, I got Devan dressed and started preparing myself. I was all dressed and starting on my hair when I decided to call Mom to make sure she was up. I heard the phone pick up, then drop to the floor. She must have been rushing, I surmised. I would call her back in a few minutes.

I continued with my hair and called back in about five minutes. Busy signal. She must be talking to one of my younger brothers. I'll give it another five minutes. I called again. Another busy signal. I called each of my brothers and got through to them. They were not talking with our mom. I panicked and told Anthony I was heading to my mom's house immediately.

I tried to stay calm as I drove. Once I got to her house, I rang the doorbell repeatedly. No answer. I banged on the door. No answer. I climbed through a bedroom window and raced to her room. She was lying on the floor with blood coming out of her mouth. There was blood on the floor around her. She was barely conscious. I called 911, and an ambulance was sent immediately. I called Anthony and explained what happened and that I was heading to the hospital.

Several hours went by before we learned that Mom had metastatic breast cancer that had spread to her liver. She was dying. I got to see my mom in the emergency room. "Do you know who that is?" the nurse asked. "Yes. That's my daughter, Tracy," my mom responded with a weak smile. Those would be the last words she would say to me. She died four days later as I held her hand, my husband and two younger brothers by my side.

I took two weeks off from work. I was devastated. My best friend, my mother, was gone. She never let on that she was sick. She never told me. I felt betrayed by her and by God. My father had just died three years earlier, and Mom was just getting back on her feet. My brothers were suffering, and I was the oldest, the leader. I had promised my mom that I "got this" as she slipped away. I had a commitment to keep. And I had a three-month-old baby girl to care for. What do I do? Where do I turn? Back to what I do well: work.

I dove into work—headfirst—burying my pain. Fortunately, or unfortunately, I had a big project on my plate. It was a precarious situation, where a line of business was struggling to meet regulatory requirements and was bleeding money. The pressure was high, and there were mounting problems on every front. Senior management was highly engaged and overseeing every aspect of the turnaround.

My work was a developmental dream come true, right when I needed it. I was learning new things daily. The stakes and pressure were incredibly high, and I loved it. I was thriving! Or so I thought.

What started out as a normal forty-hour-a-week role quickly evolved into fifty to sixty hours a week. I was working long hours, getting to work around 8:30 in the morning, and leaving no earlier than 7:00 p.m. Many evenings I left work after 8:00 p.m. The harder and longer I worked, the more progress our team made on the issues, and the less time I had to think about losing my mother—or about being a mother.

The twelve-hour days went on for a few weeks. I reasoned that if I got home and got Devan to bed before Anthony came home from work, I was doing a good job. I was meeting my obligations at work, and I was taking care of my child, right? Devan was with family while I was at work, which was just as good as being with me, right? Everyone was winning: me, my job, my child.

One Friday night, Anthony came home from work shortly after I had put Devan to bed for the night. Empty baby bottle in hand, I met him in the kitchen as he came in the back door. He asked when I had gotten home. I answered truthfully—I had worked until 9:00 and did not get home with Devan until after 10:00. He knew I had worked late before, but never this late. He was furious.

"What are you doing?" he asked in shock. I had no answer. "Our child needs you," he continued. "I know your work is important, but she's more important. You need to figure it out because this is unacceptable." He was right.

I knew that I needed to make a change. My actions were not lining up with my values and priorities. I had so much depending upon me, but I wasn't sure I could handle it all. I was the new matriarch of the family, and my brothers were looking to me for guidance and a shoulder to cry on. My work, which I loved, was high-paced and high-stress. Our daughter was not yet six months old, and I had no idea what I was doing as a mother. I was overwrought with grief and could not imagine facing it and surviving. I knew I had to face my feelings and stop using work to hide. I had to pull it together, so this moment in time would make me stronger and not take me out altogether.

Living in Authentic Alignment

There will likely be times in your career when life throws everything at you. For me, it was death, birth, and new career opportunities, all at the same time. While your story may not play out exactly the same way mine did, you will be tried by your own crucible moments: moments when you are challenged, and you struggle to survive, somehow transformed, for the better, by the experience. The catalyst that drives the transformation to a better you is authentic alignment. Here's how you do it.

Know your values. Ask yourself right now: What is most important to me? What do I value most in my life? List your top three values. These should be what matter most to you and not what society or others say you should value. Values can change over time, but we must always check in with ourselves from time to time to understand what means the most to us. Consider values in the areas of spirituality, family, health and wellbeing, friendships, and work. Make it an annual exercise to check in on your values, maybe at the beginning of the year or when you set goals. Don't wait until a crucible moment comes along to knock you off balance.

Check your priorities. How do you spend your time? How much of your time is dedicated to work? How much is dedicated to the things you value most? Review how you prioritize your time and compare it to the time spent on your values. Is there a disconnect?

Close the gap. Here comes the hard part. Once you see the disconnect between your values and your priorities, how do you close the gap? Let me give you a few ideas to help you.

Tip #1: Get some perspective. Realize that life is a journey with lots of seasons. When we're in our crucible moments, we see no end. But our children won't be babies forever. The huge project at work will end in six months. Apply a lens of perspective when you are developing solutions to close your alignment gap.

Tip #2: Seek support and empower others. Surviving a crucible moment all alone is not going to get you extra points at the pearly gates! Plus, it's not fun. As a leader at home and at work, reach out to others. Let them know what you need from them and empower them to take ownership.

Tip #3: Be flexible. The goal is to create the authentic life and career you love. Some days will be better than others. Sometimes you'll need to work late. Other times, you'll get home on time or even early. At the end of it all, if you can say honestly and with integrity that you did your absolute best to live your values, you're likely creating an authentic life you love.

Tip #4: Speak your truth. Many will see the changes you are making and not understand your motivation. Why are you now leaving work earlier or sending someone else to the meetings in your place? In the absence of information, humans make it up—and the story that fills this absence is almost always worse than the truth. As a leader, you want to drive the narrative about you, your leadership, and your career. Share your story. As always, it empowers you and other women.

Authenticity in Action

Sometimes my coaching is delivered in single but deep sessions with women to help them think through their crucible moment to land on an authentic path forward. Such was the case with Ms. R. An executive in a male-dominated field, Ms. R was about to have her first child, and she was concerned about how to balance her career with her new responsibilities as a parent. As her due date approached, she was worried about how her life would change and how those changes would impact her career possibilities.

Recently promoted, Ms. R shared, "My manager has been great. He promoted me, and my career is finally moving in the direction I want. But I'm concerned about how much time to take off for maternity leave. If I'm gone for too long, I'm afraid I'll throw off my career progress."

"Let's get some perspective, first," I said. "Maternity leave is twelve weeks, max, right? You were just recently promoted, and you've got some momentum on your career and more goals that you want to achieve over the next couple of years. Correct?" She responded positively to both.

I asked, "What matters most to you over the next year?"

"Getting bonded with our child is what matters most," she replied definitively.

"How can you use the twelve weeks you have available to focus on what matters most? Do you want to take the entire twelve weeks, or would some other amount of time allow you to put your child first then gradually shift some of your focus back to work? What would work best for you? How can you comfortably navigate this moment, focusing on your priorities?" I asked.

"Maybe I can take ten weeks of leave?" she stated.

"What is the key to keeping your career going through those ten weeks?" I asked.

"I guess it would be keeping my work front and center with my manager and not dropping any balls," she said thoughtfully.

"How can you get your team engaged to help you with that?" I asked. Ms. R shared that she could begin to transition some of her responsibilities to someone on her team and would talk her plan over with her manager for his support.

Ms. R and her husband landed on six weeks of maternity leave. She returned to work happy and back into excelling at her role. When she and I caught up months later, Ms. R shared that she had done what felt right for her, honoring her values and gaining a new perspective on how to focus on both family and work. She was now a working mother who had expanded her authenticity by embracing the role in a way that worked best for her.

Authenticity is often refined during crisis moments. You can't plan these moments, but you don't have to fear or avoid them. Jumping completely into one aspect of your life—work or home— and forsaking the other is not the answer either. The best answer is working from the inside out, using your authenticity to create alignment.

Authenticity Lessons & Reflections

1. **Don't shy away from crucible moments. These moments provide tremendous opportunities for growth.** *What challenges are you facing that may force you to change? What changes are you hesitant to make, and why? What skill or quality can you refine or develop in this challenging time?*

2. **Instead of work-life balance, focus on living in authentic alignment.** *What are your values? What will define your life experiences? Are your actions aligned to your values? If not, what needs to change?*

3. **Look to those who can support you during your crucible moments.** *Who can support you best in this moment? How can they help you during this challenging time? What do you need from each of them?*

CHAPTER 5

SHOULD WHAT HAPPENS AT HOME, STAY AT HOME?

For quite a while, my answer to this question would have been a definite "Yes!" But the path to an authentic career is created from countless moments of authenticity. Many of those moments will be driven from a place of strength. Some of those moments will be driven by vulnerability. Make no mistake, though, the moments of vulnerability will be some of your most powerful opportunities to expand your authenticity and your impact.

I was raised by two loving parents who were married for twenty-eight years until death split them apart. My loving parents were also alcoholics who many days struggled to just complete the normal tasks of raising a family of three children. There were ups and downs, embarrassing moments, proud moments, and everything in between.

There were periods of sobriety and normalcy. And there were periods of intoxication when things were far from normal. During those days of drinking and abnormality, my father would warn us kids not to disclose what went on at the house on the hill. "What happens at 5726 (our address), stays at 5726!" he would bark in his drunkenness. I learned at a very young age to keep my personal life to myself, until one day I didn't. I couldn't. The power of vulnerability was too strong.

I had been in leadership for a couple of years. My team was growing, and one of the women, who was relatively new to management, was struggling with one of her associates. After a few belligerent outbursts from the associate, several challenges with her performance, and late returns from lunch smelling like alcohol, we surmised that this associate had a drinking problem. One more behavior or performance issue would be her last. Termination was imminent.

My office door was open when my new manager rushed in. "I just had another run-in with her. We've got to do something. She's disruptive, unproductive, and now insubordinate," she exclaimed. I went over to the door and closed it. My manager was exasperated as she spoke, "I'll call HR. We'll have to let her go. I can't manage her, and it's not fair to the others on the team. They're having a hard time working with her. Nobody wants to work with her."

"Let me talk to her," I said. For some reason, I felt it wasn't time to give up on her.

"Maybe if she hears from you, she'll take things seriously," the manager said as she left my office.

About ten minutes later, I was sitting next to the woman. I can't remember how the conversation got started, but it didn't take long for me to reach a turning point. I was going to defy my father's rule. I was going to share an ugly secret that very few knew. "I am a child of alcoholic parents," I stated.

She stared at me, wide-eyed, as her mouth dropped open slowly. I knew she was mother to a teenaged son. I heard myself explaining that I understood what it felt like to be a child in an alcoholic home—the emotional instability, the unsafe feelings, the overwhelming responsibility to be an adult in the house when the adults weren't capable.

I was bringing what happened at home right into the office! Was I revealing too much? Was I crossing a line that I would later regret? But it felt so right to share that piece of myself. What would happen if others found out? What would my team think of me? Would I be viewed as an emotionally scarred leader? Would every decision I made in the past and henceforth be evaluated for some hidden, underlying meaning linked to my childhood? But the dirty deed was done, and it felt good. It felt good to be vulnerable if it helped someone be better.

We talked for some time and agreed that the best course of action was to contact HR and our employee assistance program to get help. She ultimately went on leave for several weeks. She returned to work and thanked me for helping her and not firing her. She became a productive associate again.

The Vulnerability-Power Line

My first act of vulnerability was totally unplanned, and boy, was it powerful! I realized that when I looked to the breadth of my life—and not just the life I had created at work—I had so much more to draw upon to connect with the people I was leading.

Why did I share my secret? To deny that moment of connection would have meant missing an opportunity to motivate someone to be better. It could have meant firing a valuable employee. It also would have meant denying a part of myself, being inauthentic.

Authenticity demands vulnerability. Being vulnerable means that you are willing to take a risk when you have no control over the outcome. Leaders often don't want to feel vulnerable because they don't want to portray any weakness that may be perceived as an indication that they are not worthy of leading people.

Many leaders want to appear all-knowing, wise, prepared, and always in control. For women and minority women leaders, being vulnerable is like stepping off a precipice and not knowing if you'll live or die. Most would rather bury their truth than reveal it and risk an uncertain outcome. Why is this?

When you are a woman or minority woman in leadership in a corporate environment, you don't often see many others like you in similar positions. This becomes ever more painfully true the higher you progress up the corporate ladder. When most of the people around you in leadership are male and/or white, as a woman or minority, you are not considered the norm.

You likely do not look like the majority, and given that our experiences drive our perspectives, as a woman or minority woman, you likely have unique perspectives on issues that may differ from the majority.

Being vulnerable can mean sharing something that stands out as different from the norm. It can mean acknowledging that you don't know something, or it can mean acknowledging you do know something from a prior experience that may be perceived as out of the ordinary. When you are vulnerable, you risk revealing something that might make you appear more different or less like the norm—less like what is expected and somehow less valuable. Being vulnerable can mean taking a huge risk.

When you practice authenticity, being vulnerable generates power and adds value. Vulnerability is about allowing all aspects of who you are to shape how you lead so that your outcomes are greater than the norm. Vulnerability is honesty in action.

Authentic leaders access their vulnerability to get the most and best out of themselves and the people they work with. They tap into the full breadth of their experiences to lead. They realize that we all are shaped by our experiences, that experiences can inform our actions, and that when we combine our experience and knowledge with that of others, we become more powerful.

Authentic leaders know that denying some aspect of who they are requires energy—and that becomes energy that isn't available to draw upon for being our best. It's wasted energy, lost power. Why not use every bit of who you are to be a better leader? Why not learn to walk the vulnerability-power line?

Being vulnerable enhances your authentic leadership brand. It makes you human and connects you to people of all levels. It's an equalizer. Sometimes being vulnerable is as simple as acknowledging when we don't have the answer. Vulnerability can be expressed by supporting someone on your team to take the lead on challenging work and giving them the space and support to fail, learn, and keep going forward.

Vulnerability builds trust, and trust empowers a leader and her team to greater success by connecting people together more tightly. People who trust one another are more likely to go into battle together and weather a storm together. Trust is the solid foundation that sustains teams in difficult times.

Authenticity in Action

Many years after that first vulnerability moment, I sat at the back of the room, waiting for the guest speaker at a leadership development program to start. This speaker—I'll call her Ms. C—was one of my favorite people to work with. I had met her a few years before when my team was looking for executives to help sponsor our resource groups.

She had been recommended to me by a close colleague who warned, "Ms. C has a fabulous story, but she doesn't like to share it much internally. I'll send you a copy of an article that was written about her in a local newspaper. She's fabulous. Good luck getting her to engage. She tends to just focus on the work and not make too much out of her story."

I had made a trip, along with a colleague, to Ms. C's office. You could feel the energy she radiated. People were drawn to her. Her team loved her. And they were a winning team that was getting great results. Her leadership was empowering others to grow, and their business was thriving.

We had discussed resource groups and the opportunity for her to be a co-sponsor. I shared that I had read her story. "It's a powerful story," I told her. "You should be telling that story to as many of our associates as possible. You can empower others to become strong leaders." Ms. C was reluctant to commit to anything right then, but a bond was formed between the two of us that day. We stayed connected, coaching and supporting each other as we fought to stay true to ourselves and drive change in the corporate environment.

Ms. C had quietly continued doing great work for the company. Eventually, when the call was made, she agreed to share her story with these developing leaders. A naturally gifted storyteller, Ms. C shared her journey from a child who lived in poverty, to a young woman who served in the military, to a college graduate who defied those who told her she would never amount to anything, to a leader of a multi-million- dollar line of business in a Fortune 500 company.

Once she finished, a long line formed to chat with her. I stood nearby, observing and listening as she was thanked by so many who appreciated her authenticity and those who wanted more tips on how to be a better leader.

Six months later, I would serve as the guest speaker at Ms. C's leadership summit. As I eased into the back of the room quietly about fifteen minutes before I was scheduled to speak, she came up and encircled me with a huge bear hug, her signature. "What's your favorite song these days?" she asked in a whisper so as not to interrupt the current speaker.

"I don't know," I whispered, caught off guard.

"What about Bruno Mars?" she continued, not missing a beat. "I need some entry music for you," she explained.

"Entry music?" I thought to myself. I love to dance, but I wasn't completely comfortable with making a grand entrance to the beat of music. How seriously would my audience take my message if I spent the first couple of minutes dancing? But I trusted Ms. C. And I had encouraged her to be vulnerable and share her story. It was time to take a chance.

The break came as the other speaker finished. Bruno Mars' *24K Magic* came on as I strutted to the front of the room to the beat of the music with her by my side. We got to the front of the room and danced together, bumping hips. The crowd clapped to the beat and laughed at our dancing.

The music stopped, and she introduced me gracefully. The energy was palpable. I went on to deliver my speech about diversity, inclusion, and ways leaders can mitigate bias. The engagement from the room was remarkable. This was a tough topic for a room that was mostly male and overwhelmingly white. This was a leadership summit with her unique stamp on it—from the music to the speakers to the topics of discussion.

Ms. C had created something special by her willingness to be vulnerable and share herself with others on a personal level. She risked ridicule, not being taken seriously, and resistance. But in the end, her vulnerability created connection and engagement.

How to Walk Your Vulnerability-Power Line

Tapping into your vulnerability is a very personal decision. Sometimes that decision happens in an instant, and other times, it evolves over time. No matter how it happens, it's unique to you.

Often, we try to draw a clean, clear line between who we are at work and who we are at home, when who we are is truly a result of all our experiences. Just as you can't forget your name when at work, you can't forget your experiences outside of work. They are always with you because they form your knowledge base. And knowledge never goes away. How much to share, when to share, and why you share are the keys to finding your personal vulnerability-power line.

It's all about balance. Here are some tips on how to walk the line.

Maintain your position. As a leader, being vulnerable is not about forgetting your role as a leader to connect with those you lead. Don't abdicate your position, even for a second, to make yourself or others comfortable. It's not about being less, stepping back, or being different. It's about giving people clear visibility into an aspect of who you are or what you know. Your leadership is a prominent piece of who you are.

Frame your story. Vulnerability is not about a total dump of your story or knowledge on people. It's about connecting your story or knowledge to the situation at hand. Put forward what connects to others or to the situation, not more, not less. Present your truth in a way that you can always own in the environment you're navigating. If what you share gets retold by others, how will it play? Will it alienate you?

Seek always to add value. Opening up to share personal knowledge or experiences is best when it adds value, insight, or clarification. Any other use may appear self-serving. Will it be relevant to the situation or sound like useless noise, bragging, or gossip? Nothing in your story is off-limits, but not everything is relevant.

Tell your universal truth. Being vulnerable is not about placing a mask on or off as needed. It's about sharing relevant truth and being authentic. Your truth is infinite, meaning it never goes away. It's universal for you. When you choose to be vulnerable, you should never feel that you are removing your work mask to wear your personal mask. You should never feel that you are switching your language, behavior, or expression to be accepted or to gain advantage. Vulnerability may feel uncomfortable, but it should never feel fake. When you choose to be vulnerable, you are allowing people a peek at a piece of your universal truth.

Vulnerability is a way to supercharge your power at work. When you tap into vulnerability, two immensely powerful things happen. First, you demonstrate your humanity by your willingness to share personal knowledge or experiences. Humanity establishes connection. This enables people to see themselves through your experiences. This is incredibly powerful for other women and minority women who aspire to higher levels of achievement, as it gives them a role model, someone they can see who exemplifies what they hope to be someday. It's incredibly powerful for the teams you lead because they are motivated to achieve in support of the connection you have made with them by trusting them with your story. It engages them in a more personal way.

Second, your vulnerability establishes psychological safety among your team or your peers. When people feel safe, they are more likely to engage fully and share ideas and information—good and bad—in a less-filtered way, without fear of criticism, shame, or retribution of some sort. This will give you access to richer information, which leads to better decision-making. You become a more effective leader.

Authenticity can be ironic. Sometimes to be authentic, we draw strength from being willing to share our perceived weakness. By giving up some control and power over outcomes and perceptions, we gain power in our leadership. Vulnerability is a tremendous source of authentic power. Vulnerability is authentic courage in action.

Authenticity Lessons & Reflections

1. **Access your vulnerability to add value.** *When have you chosen not to be vulnerable? Why? How could your vulnerability have added value? What would you do differently?*

2. **Own your universal truth. We can't divorce ourselves from our challenging work or personal life experiences.** *Reflect on the challenging experiences you have had. What have you learned? How do those experiences shape your leadership? How can they shape your career?*

3. **Learn to frame your story.** *What relevant experiences have you not shared for fear of being vulnerable? How can you bring your story to others in an authentic way?*

CHAPTER 6

RESPECT YOURSELF

Organizations are usually based on a hierarchy. We all report to someone. Typically, the higher one goes up the hierarchy, the greater the level of responsibility and authority. Sometimes we let authority, responsibility, or hierarchy cause us to be less than authentic or to accept behavior that dishonors us. Remember, self-respect comes first. It's a prerequisite for authenticity. Like many of you, I've been challenged by this at times in my career.

An example of this was an uncomfortable meeting I once sat in. I glanced at my watch, 5:00, and we were only halfway through our list of project updates. Slow, quiet, sigh. Another late evening on the books. My colleague across the table was flushing, her cheeks a bright pink. She was up next to provide updates. Was it nerves or the stuffy, hot room?

I guessed it was nerves. We were working for one of the most challenging leaders in the organization. Ms. R, a vice president who reported directly to the regional CEO, had high expectations and an unrelenting push for perfection. She could be a beast under the best circumstances. And these were not the best circumstances. This was our second meeting of the week, and it was only Wednesday.

I listened intently and took notes as my colleagues provided their updates, and we made our way down the project list. My turn would be soon. I was feeling surprisingly good, all things considered. My list of operational issues was long, and I had prioritized the work by ROI, bottom-line impact, and time to correct. My team had made great progress on all the top priorities in less than five business days.

It was finally time to provide my update, and I ran through my list efficiently. As I finished, Ms. R asked about one item. It was the item that was last on my list because bottom-line impact was minimal, it would take a long time to implement, and it was no longer a required process.

I had instructed my team not to focus on this item as a priority. Their time was more valuably spent on the other priorities. As I was explaining this, Ms. R cut me off, "We meet so that we can stay on top of everything. Everything. We discussed this item at our last meeting, and I expected an update today. Is there a reason why you haven't made any progress on this item?"

I felt my cheeks go hot. I thought I had answered that question effectively already. I fumbled for words and replied, "This item will create an expense, with little to no benefit. With so many higher, more valuable priorities and limited resources, I thought it was best to prioritize it lower on the list and tackle it later."

"But we specifically talked about this in our last meeting! It's on the list for a reason! If you're going to take something off the list, you need to talk to me first," she replied, glaring at me. I could feel the discomfort of my colleagues as they sat quietly and observed, so happy it was not one of them who was being interrogated. As I opened my mouth to explain that I was not taking it off the list, just reprioritizing, Ms. R cut me off and abruptly spit out the words, "Let's take a break."

The table cleared immediately, and I sat stunned for three seconds before I gathered myself and left the meeting room to find another conference room with a phone. I dialed into the voicemail system and recorded a clear, brief message in as positive a voice as I could muster: "Hi, this is Tracy. I am extremely uncomfortable with the tone of our conversation in our update meeting today. I didn't like how it made me feel. I'd like to discuss it with you. I'll reach out to your assistant and schedule a brief meeting, hopefully, for this week. I look forward to talking. Thanks." I scheduled delivery of the call for later that evening and entered Ms. R's office number. We regrouped, and the meeting continued for the next hour. After it was over, I went home, drained of my energy and commitment.

Later that week, on Friday, I met with Ms. R in her office. After a few minutes of polite conversation, she began, "I'm glad you called. I didn't realize I had made you uncomfortable. That was not my intention at all," she offered.

"I was embarrassed by the conversation," I said.

She sat back in her chair, surprised. "I'm sorry," she said. I did not mean to embarrass you."

I responded, "I felt like you did not trust my decision-making and that you didn't value the work and progress my team had made on some important items. I'd like to understand my responsibilities and what I may need to do differently."

"You are doing a good job," she interjected with sincerity, leaning forward. I could tell she didn't realize how I and others perceived her behavior.

Ms. R and I spent the next hour discussing the project. We came to a clear understanding about decision-making and prioritization. I was clear about and satisfied with the role I would play. I owned my space, and it gave me the opportunity to grow in my leadership. The intense meetings continued, but there were no more embarrassing moments for me.

Authentically Owning Your Space

You often hear the term "owning your space" when people talk about executive presence. It's typically a reference to the verbal and non-verbal cues that one gives in meetings or presentations or in other opportunities to be present with your colleagues or other executives.

When you own your space, you show up with a confidence that says you deserve to be present, and you know what you are doing. But authentically owning your space is more than just how you show up physically in an environment. Authentic ownership of your space starts with the expectations and boundaries you set about how you will be engaged and treated as an individual, employee, and leader. It begins with mentally reframing the employer-employee relationship.

Reframe the Employer-Employee Relationship

Have you ever heard a leader introduce her team members by saying, "she works for me"? That has always made me uncomfortable because it implied a level of ownership and hierarchy that can signal value and power.

It's important—both as a leader and as an employee—to remember that we work for companies, not our leaders. We report to our leaders. We work **for** the customers and shareholders, and we work **with** others—our direct reports, our peers, and our leaders.

There's no implied ownership between employee and manager, but instead, all of us are connected through common goals and objectives. Does this mean we don't respect the authority of our leaders? Absolutely not. What it does mean is that our contribution is valuable no matter what role we play.

The employer-employee relationship is a social contract based on exchange of value. People contribute their value through work in exchange for payment, accomplishment, development, social contribution, many things. Organizations exist based on the value they offer their customers through their employees.

It always comes down to value, but sometimes the concept is lost. Hierarchy can create misperceptions about value. Hierarchy can lead us to believe that the CEO is more valuable than the front-line employee.

Value is relative. The CEO is valuable for her contributions (e.g., working with the board, establishing strategic direction, communicating to the market and shareholders), and the front-line associate is valuable for their contributions (e.g., handling customer calls, processing claims, enrolling members).

Is one more valuable than another? The reality is that a good organization needs both. When we reframe the employer-employee relationship to one of value exchange, we can hold firm to our expectations and boundaries about how we will be treated as an individual, employee, and leader.

What are those expectations and boundaries? You must establish your own expectations and boundaries in the workplace, but there are some basics to always keep in mind and never sacrifice.

Individual (personal) Expectations and Boundaries: Individual expectations and boundaries are set based on your personal values and your basic rights as an individual. Safety at work is a great example of an individual expectation that is a basic right. A more personal expectation could be not using foul language in work interactions.

Employee Expectations and Boundaries: Your employee expectations build upon your personal, individual expectations and boundaries, and they include rights you have as an employee. Employee expectations can include being respected for your contribution and for the skills, talents, and experiences you bring to your role. Expecting to be paid equally for equal work is a basic employee right and expectation.

Leader Expectations and Boundaries: Leader expectations and boundaries build upon our expectations as an employee and can be as unique as the leader. For example, as a leader, it is reasonable to expect transparency from other leaders with whom you work. It is reasonable to expect to be your own messenger for communicating with your team or to others on matters impacting your team. Many organizations will articulate specific leadership expectations. While these help to shape the culture, it's important that you also know what you expect as a leader and where your boundaries lie. For example, as a leader, it was important to me that my decision-making authority be respected from above and below. And when I felt that I was treated in a way that dishonored my boundaries, I made sure that I had a conversation to clarify expectations of my role.

Failure to address violations of our boundaries puts us out of integrity with ourselves. Sometimes, at work, for the sake of keeping our job or out of perceived respect for authority, we don't address boundary violations. It's detrimental to ourselves on two fronts: we're not living authentically when we're out of integrity with ourselves, and we teach others how to treat us by the boundaries and expectations we hold.

When you fail to align on expectations and boundaries, you are inviting the violator to unknowingly, or possibly knowingly, continue behavior that is upsetting to you. Owning our space means not just having boundaries and expectations but living to them and taking the action necessary to ensure that they are respected. That's the difficult part! Sometimes you must make career-changing decisions to live authentically.

Authenticity in Action

It's often said that people don't leave companies; they leave bad managers. I was thinking about this idea as I headed into the exit interview meeting with one of our women executives, Ms. T.

"So, tell me about this great opportunity," I asked her excitedly.

"Well, it's not a promotion. But I will have the autonomy to direct my team, and that's incredibly exciting!" she beamed. "It's here in the city, doing the same work I do here. The company is much smaller, so my team will not be as large, but that doesn't concern me." She smiled as she spoke, excitement radiating from her.

I put my cards on the table: "What can we do to keep you here? We don't want to lose you. You know that, right?" I explained.

"There's nothing you can do. We tried everything, remember? I love what I do, but I can't do it here the way I'd like to. It took me a long time to accept that. I've been here almost ten years. But I'm willing to make a change."

As Ms. T spoke, I reflected on when we met a couple of years prior. As her HR business partner, we had established a coaching relationship.

The key issue we worked on was respect from her manager for her leadership. She was an executive and had no goals for ascending higher and no desire to work in another function. Ms. T loved what she did, and she was good at it. But her love for her role changed dramatically with a new manager.

When her new leader came on board, there was an unspoken change in expectations. Her new leader became highly engaged in her function, even calling Ms. T's direct reports and unintentionally overriding her direction several times.

In our coaching sessions, we worked through how to have a conversation with her manager about Ms. T's expectations for her own role as a leader. Ms. T expected to have accountability for directing her team. She was totally open to changes in direction from her new leader, but she wanted to own communicating those changes to her team directly.

Her manager simply loved to engage directly with all members of the leadership team, including those that reported to his direct reports. There was no intention of undermining Ms. T's authority, and she knew that, but those conversations with her direct reports often led to creative ideas and changes in direction without Ms. T's involvement.

In one of our coaching conversations, Ms. T explained with an exasperated tone, "I'm flexible. My manager's ideas are not bad. I just wish we could discuss them first. I'm always the last one to know, and I don't feel my role is respected. In fact, I'm not sure my manager even needs me here. What's the point? I've already been a doer in my career. Now is my time to lead. I'm an executive, for goodness sake! I'm not even earning my salary!"

Ms. T and I discussed options for handling the situation. First, she needed to communicate her understanding of her responsibilities as a leader, her expectations of what it meant for her to lead, and reach an agreement with her manager about what that would look like. Then, they could decide the role that Ms. T and her manager would each play in leading the team. While they reached a verbal agreement several times, it was difficult for Ms. T's manager to put those words in action consistently.

The second option was for her to pursue other roles in the company, which didn't appeal to Ms. T. The third option, which was not a real option for Ms. T, was to change her own expectations of her role and to accept the approach of her new manager. This was a hard "no" for Ms. T because she had grown in her leadership and had clear expectations for her role. For her, being a leader meant owning decisions and not being overridden without consultation. That was a hard boundary.

The last option, which she ultimately pursued, was to find another, similar role elsewhere. While this was a difficult moment for me personally, seeing a talented leader leave our company, it was an empowering moment. Ms. T had taken ownership of her space. She had acknowledged and communicated her expectations, and when her leader overstepped Ms. T's boundary, she worked through solutions.

Her excitement about her new role wasn't just excitement about a new adventure. It was excitement from taking ownership of her authenticity. Her actions lined up with who she wanted to be as a leader, and in acting, she demonstrated the ultimate respect—respect for herself.

To create an authentic career, we must start with self-respect for our own boundaries and expectations. When you own your space, grounded by the value you inherently bring to your role, you are choosing authenticity over structure, hierarchy, or role. Your opportunities are limitless.

Authenticity Lessons & Reflections

1. **Authenticity at work requires a courageous relationship with our self.** *When have you been most courageous at work? What were the circumstances? How did you feel after being courageous? What did you learn about yourself?*

2. **Owning your space requires that you own your value and stand respectfully in your expectations and boundaries.** *Identify a few of your individual, employee, and leadership boundaries. When have your boundaries or expectations been dishonored by someone with higher positional authority? How can you use courage and respect to address the issue?*

3. **Owning your space with peers may come in the form of challenges to your responsibilities or knowledge.** *When have your responsibilities or knowledge been challenged by colleagues? How well did you own your space? What did you do well? What was challenging?*

CHAPTER 7

GRACE UNDER PRESSURE

Carbon under pressure transforms into either a sparkly diamond or a lump of coal. This transformation is pretty straightforward. Carbon with impurities turns into coal when placed under pressure, while pure carbon placed under pressure becomes a diamond. Why are we talking about carbon and pressure? Because believe it or not, humans respond to pressure in similar ways.

Challenges and stressful events create pressure that can transform us into either our best or worst selves—a diamond or a lump of coal. The difference is that we can choose how we respond to outside pressure. Ideally, we stay pure and true to ourselves by maintaining authentic grace under pressure, which transforms us into the diamonds we are meant to be.

Daily Challenges

As working women leaders, pressure is a way of life. While pressure is an expected part of our daily schedules, we should also recognize that it's built into the corporate structure. As a married-with-three-kids, African American woman executive in a Fortune 30 company, I was an anomaly in the corporate world, and that added to the pressure! Let's consider what women face as they climb the corporate ladder.

It starts with our paychecks. According to EqualPayToday.org, based on 2019 U.S. Census data, women earned $0.82 cents for every dollar earned by white males. Black women earned $0.62. The situation is even worse for Native American and Latina women who earned $0.60 and $0.55, respectively.[2]

The next challenge involves finding female leaders, mentors, and peers. According to Catalyst, in 2019, women made up just 5.8 percent of the CEOs in the S&P 500 companies and 26.5 percent of executives and senior-level officials/managers. They held only 21.2 percent of corporate board seats. Yet, women were 44.7 percent of the total S&P 500 employees.[3]

You get the picture. We want success, but it feels like the odds are against us, especially when we look at our environment and what the data clearly shows we're up against.

These corporate pressures on women get turned up a notch when we have challenges at work—poor operational performance, challenging employees, sales losses, low revenue, technology breakdowns, etc.

No woman wants to let work challenges turn her into the CEO of Bitch Inc! Instead, we have to develop effective strategies to manage and respond to external pressures. Simultaneously, these solutions need to stay true to our authentic selves.

---

[2] "Overview 2020 – Equal Pay Today," Equal Pay Today! accessed September 25, 2020, http://www.equalpaytoday.org/equalpaydays.

[3] "Pyramid: Women in S&P 500 Companies | Catalyst (January 15, 2020)," Catalyst, accessed September 25, 2020, https://www.catalyst.org/research/women-in-sp-500-companies/.

Reacting Versus Responding

How we handle daily and corporate pressure impacts not only our job performance but also our mental health. Specifically, what we do during stressful situations can make all the difference. Do we react or respond? It may seem like I'm splitting hairs, but there's a difference between reacting and responding to a situation.

Reactions are automatic. We're on autopilot when we react. In contrast, responses are thoughtful. Responses incorporate space for a pause, no matter how brief. During that moment, we tap into our intellect, then connect with our feelings before answering. (Sometimes, the pause is nanoseconds. Sometimes, it's overnight. Both are okay.)

Reactions are often emotionally driven. Similar to carbon with impurities under pressure, the emotions "dirty" our answer to a challenge. As a result, the objective or solution we're trying to communicate often gets lost in the emotion of a reaction.

While responses often include emotion, thought intercedes and channels the emotion in a way that enhances and clarifies the point. Similar to pure carbon under pressure, responses allow us to maintain "purity" in our answer by pushing us to take a moment to pause and think. A response combines initial emotions with reflection. Combining emotions with reflection can help effectively communicate our ideas and gracefully demonstrate our authenticity.

Does this mean we strip away our emotions when we respond to challenging situations? Absolutely not! Emotion makes us human. It's an essential part of authenticity, and it has an important place. But emotion at work should be applied like salt to food—just enough enhances flavor, too much ruins the meal.

Use emotion to emphasize what is important. Use it to motivate and to stir others to action. Use it to connect with the people you lead.

Use it to show urgency. Use it to show how much you care. But always take a moment to pause, reflect, and then respond so that you use emotion wisely for a positive outcome. Own it and put it to work for you when responding. When we simply react, the emotion owns us.

> **Reaction = Emotion – Reflection**
> **Response = Emotion + Reflection**

Lump of Coal Moments

All of us have what I like to call "ugly lump of coal moments," but these uncomfortable moments are important because they connect us to how we authentically feel. They teach us how to channel our emotions. One of my lump of coal moments came from a building frustration about a critical project's slow progress.

A lot was at stake. A highly regulated line of business had been mismanaged for years, and we were on the brink of a big financial loss as well as government intervention. I was working with senior management daily, and their expectations were high, almost unrealistically high. They expected an immediate operations turnaround. Senior management was under pressure, and I was feeling the pressure, too. Doing this project well would be important for my career.

With these thoughts running through my mind, I sat in my office waiting as my management team trickled in for a status meeting. We moved quickly down our list of open items until we reached carryover topics from the last meeting.

At this point, one of the managers explained, "I haven't had a chance to call about this yet. As soon as we leave this meeting, I'll make the call."

I was livid. I screamed inside, "Make the time to call!" Not only was this item dragging on too long, but it was the third item that didn't have a clear resolution. I could hear my heart beating in my ears and thought to myself, "Why don't they understand how important this is?"

I turned to the manager and glared at her. "Do I need to make this call?" I heard myself say aloud. I could see the embarrassment on her face. I felt out of control and afraid. I was relying on others to get the work done, but somehow, they lacked the same sense of urgency as me.

Before she could speak, I lashed out, "I'm not sure what the hell is going on here, but we've got do better than this. Problems need to be solved faster than this!"

I struggled to find words that were longer than four letters, and finding none, I rose from my chair, strode across the room, and left my office, slamming the door behind me, down two flights of stairs and out the back door of the building to the parking lot. I walked around the building several times to calm down.

"How embarrassing!" I thought as I walked. "I've never lost my cool like this. I'm usually so good under pressure. I've always been calm in a crisis. What is wrong with me? This is not me. How do I make this right?"

Twenty minutes later, I slowly opened the door to my office and went back to my chair. The team glanced up from their conversation and immediately turned back to their work as if to say, "Oh, it's you." I sat quietly like an outsider watching them work. They reviewed a couple of updates with me—sharing that they had made the call and had clear next steps on the open issue. We finished up, and the team left my office, chatting quietly among themselves. No one said a word about my meltdown that day or since.

Channel Emotions Authentically

Over the next few weeks, I thought a lot about my actions. Being able to walk away under pressure and leave the problems to others was a real luxury of being the boss. My team couldn't walk away. They certainly couldn't storm out of a meeting with the boss when they were frustrated.

Ultimately, I understood that my direction had failed to provide the team with the right sense of urgency. I had disconnected my powerful emotion—fear—from my actions. I was engaging my team without appropriately expressing the amount of pressure I was under and the urgency of the situation. It was natural to feel anxious and afraid of taking on a project of this enormity and importance. It was inauthentic not to communicate these feelings.

Instead of holding back my fear, I could have channeled it into action. I could have communicated my expectations (and those of senior management) to my team. They would have better understood the urgency of the project, and that would have helped alleviate my concerns.

Looking back, I recognize what I could have changed, and it has helped me move forward. Strong emotions are to be expected, but we can't shy away from them. We need to identify them and then channel those feelings into appropriate actions.

The next time you feel yourself swirling in emotions, consider these steps:

Name the emotion.
Name it. Own it. What emotion is a situation creating? Is it fear? Stress? Anger? For me, it was fear.

Determine the cause.
What drives the emotion? Why are you feeling this emotion? I was afraid that my team would not get the work done fast enough to meet senior management's expectations, and I would then be viewed as ineffective.

Address the cause.
Identify what can be done to address the cause of your emotion, then channel your emotions toward a resolution that works for you. I needed to express the urgency of the work and tell my team that I would be pushing them to keep the work moving.

Expand Your Value

Grace under pressure is about more than what we say or do in a single high-pressure moment. It's about handling extended periods of pressure during which we have to both gracefully manage ourselves and effectively manage our resources and team.

Early in my career, I had the opportunity to work with a phenomenal vice president. She often reminded me, "You don't have to solve it on your own, girl!" She could see that, like many women leaders (and especially minority women leaders), I struggled most to engage others when times were tough. I would shrink inside myself to find solutions instead of expanding and reaching out to others for assistance.

Rather than shrinking in avoidance, it's important to expand our authenticity to meet the moment, especially when faced with challenging situations. Looking outside ourselves can be difficult, especially for women and minority women. It can feel like admitting weakness when we engage others to problem-solve or navigate difficult challenges.

As women, it's tempting to try to think our way out of pressure-filled situations. We don't want our male counterparts to believe we're not up for a challenge or that we're not capable. Minority women often feel extra pressure to keep their challenges to themselves or among a close-knit circle of friends. However, there's a problem with keeping big challenges to ourselves and off the radar screen. We don't stand out. Our value doesn't have an opportunity to shine. When things aren't easy, and we're managing big challenges, we can end up shrinking to avoid the risk of being seen as a failure.

This happens again and again because peers like us (women and minority women) are not openly discussing the difficulties they face. In this environment, it starts to feel natural to keep any pressure to ourselves. We don't want to be perceived as not knowing our space or appearing over-reliant on others for our success. We want to stand on our own.

But standing on your own means relying on more than your own skills, talents, and experiences. It means utilizing all the tools you have at your disposal, including the greatest tools you have—your colleagues and team.

Learning to tap into the power of the people around you expands your own value. You amplify your impact when you rely on the talents of those around you. The question is, how do you do it? How do you access the strength of others in a way that doesn't feel like you're ceding power or admitting failure? How can you authentically engage others in a way that is forthright about your needs but doesn't abdicate your leadership, strength, and authenticity?

To expand under pressure means looking for opportunity when faced with that pressure. Don't look at challenges as rough patches you need to survive. Look at them as opportunities where you can thrive and create value. Expanding isn't just delegating pieces of work to others. It's identifying which individuals and teams are capable of fulfilling your unique vision.

Expanding means magnifying your value by empowering others to create value. To make that happen, you need to:

Clearly understand the challenge you face.
Identify and understand the challenge and how it will get done. This is often more than simply delegating assignments to your team. You want to see the big picture and understand how different pieces can create a solution. Then, you'll be able to identify who can help and persuasively explain the "why" behind your request for an aggressive goal or significant time investment.

Be creative when identifying who can help solve the challenge.
Don't be afraid to call upon individuals who are not on your team. Sometimes the best help resides outside your control. You may need to negotiate for help. Do it.

Engage individuals to help by sharing your challenge and why you need assistance.
Time to get vulnerable by acknowledging you need help! Empower those helping you by connecting them to the bigger picture of why the challenge matters and their value in the process of solving it. Express your belief in them and the collective ability to get the work done.

Stay connected.

Now is the time to learn more, engage more, and communicate more. You may not have all the answers, but you are assembling the right individuals to address the challenge. Your value in the process involves orchestrating the team to get results. You are the one who understands all the moving parts—expanding your value by empowering others to create value. You are the catalyst!

Authenticity in Action

As a mentor, I support and guide my mentees at all times but especially when they encounter tough situations. We work together to find resolutions that not only solve their specific situations but also work for them—responses that reflect their authentic selves.

Ms. E was a seasoned leader who had recently transitioned to a new role. She was broadening her expertise, and the new position was totally outside her prior experience. Despite her newness to the role, the division head rightly had expectations and needed an update from her department.

Ms. E knew how to delegate, but she was struggling to trust her new team—wanting to own this work from beginning to end and not wanting to reveal that she was struggling with the newness of her responsibilities and lack of knowledge.

During a routine check-in, she described how she was stressed, overwhelmed, and, with only two weeks left to get the presentation to the division head done, worried. As we discussed what was going on and possible solutions, I asked her what would happen if she pulled in the managers on her team and enlisted their help preparing a first draft of the presentation.

"They could handle more tasks, but this is something that ultimately makes it to the head of the division. That's a lot of pressure for a manager," she responded.

I reminded her that this was a lot of pressure for her, and she still had yet to develop solid expertise in the department. We discussed how she could add value to the process if she let others help her out. In addition to her current team, she had worked with her division head in the past and understood his preferences. She knew that this project would also need help from outside her department.

As we broke things down, she started brainstorming, "My team is really busy, and there's a lot of data that I need." The wheels were turning. She realized, "I know who can pull the data, but they don't report to me. I'd have to reach out to see if they could help me."

"How could you get the right people together so you can get it off your plate and into motion?" I questioned.

"I could give each person on my team one part of the presentation to complete, then have the data person add the right data in. Maybe I could pull them together to brainstorm on recommendations to shape the presentation." She was energized.

At this point, she looked up and said, "I've got to go. I need to pull this group together and get a time scheduled today. I can go over expectations and set a timeline to get it done," she said with clarity.

Ms. E was expanding to meet her goals. My final encouragement before she left was to remind her to let her team know how she felt about this work. She needed to communicate her emotions to connect authentically with her team, which would let them know the importance of this presentation. Ms. E recognized that this was her first opportunity to represent the department, and as their new leader, she wanted to do it right.

Over the next year, Ms. E naturally encountered other challenges. While working through those, she developed relationships with key leaders and peers in other departments whom she could rely upon for feedback and problem-solving. When her department needed assistance with a backlog, she quickly expanded and reached out to one of her peers for assistance.

You, too, will encounter challenges and pressure on your path to creating an authentic career. In moments of pressure, we often lose sight of our value and allow reactions to direct decisions. Without staying grounded in our authentic value and following our authentic beliefs, we can shrink under pressure instead of expanding to add value.

Always remember: your authentic value is not defined purely by what you know or your ability to dig yourself out of a problem. The knowledge, skill, and talent we bring is the foundation upon which we create more value by engaging others in our work. Responding and expanding shows authentic confidence in action.

So, when you are tempted to fold under the pressure of corporate challenges, stay authentic, stay pure, and create your diamond moment.

You've got this! Stay authentically graceful!

Authenticity Lessons & Reflections

1.   **Demonstrating emotion is an important part of being authentic.** *What situations at work create emotion for you? When has emotion become a barrier to taking the right action? How have you used emotion to get work done?*

2.   **Your value expands when you empower others.** *What opportunities would allow you to expand? With your team? With colleagues? What value could you demonstrate by expanding more?*

3.   **Reaching out for support or assistance means you have confidence in your value.** *What is your greatest skill or talent? _____ Complete this sentence: I bring value by/ through_____.*

CHAPTER 8

FIND YOUR FOLLOWERS

Cristiano Ronaldo is the most-followed person on Instagram with over 238 million followers. Ariana Grande is not far behind with over 203 million followers. Followers are more than just numbers. Think about the people and groups you follow on social media. You're interested in what these people are doing, and you want to interact and show your support.

In the corporate world, you can also benefit from followers. There will be times in your career when you will need people who will support and advocate for you. As in social media, these people are likely to start supporting you because they are interested in you and what you do.

The goal is to turn these followers into superfans who want to engage and share with others their interest in you and what you do. Their support shows they trust you and have confidence that you are a good investment. I discovered the importance of superfan followers during a mid-career change.

It was March 2001. I had just returned to work after having a beautiful baby boy. My team was rocking and rolling and doing great work. My husband, Anthony, and I had agreed that it was time for me to pursue my MBA, a longtime dream of mine. It was perfect timing. Our oldest child was three years old, and I wanted to be fully engaged in my children's early years. I planned to enroll in a two-year MBA program that met for a full day on Saturdays.

As luck would have it, just before my MBA program began, I was reassigned to lead a major systems conversion project. These types of projects are always challenging. My role involved building and managing a new team of managers, reporting to senior management, and balancing tradeoffs between system updates and productivity.

It was a stressful temporary position that would be over when all customers migrated to the new system. Then, I'd have to find myself a new position, so I needed to do a great job to be marketable for my next opportunity.

How was I going to manage the stress of my young family, my marriage, and my education while completing a career-defining project and identifying my next job opportunity? It was time to start cultivating followers. I needed more than support. I needed authentic followers who recognized my unique talents and wanted to tell everyone about me! In the corporate world, these individuals are called sponsors, and they can make all the difference in your career.

Authentic Sponsorship: The Superfan Follower

An authentic sponsor is basically a superfan follower who likes, shares, and reposts to show their support for you. These actions let others know what you're doing and that your superfan believes so strongly in you that they want to rave about your contributions and capabilities.

People often get confused about the difference between sponsorship and mentorship. Mentors give advice and help you develop and learn more about yourself. You work with your mentor to navigate difficult situations. Sponsors, on the other hand, follow you from a distance and actively seek opportunities for you. They want to shine a spotlight on you and elevate your career. Sponsors know you and your capabilities, and they advocate for you.

While mentors can certainly serve as sponsors, and vice versa, do not overlook the relevance of sponsorship. Sponsors should elevate or expand your career through influence or positional authority. They bring you greater credibility and are able to make things happen for you.

Sponsors let everyone know they're superfan followers because they let others know what you're doing. Their support is heard at talent meetings and shared at project updates and staff meetings. A sponsor serves as your number one superfan!

Sponsorship is a critical aspect of career development, especially for women and minority women who aspire to leadership and increasing responsibility. Because it is challenging for women and women of color to break through to the top leadership roles, having someone sponsor them helps to provide access to opportunities that may happen slowly or not at all without a sponsor who advocates for them. Sponsorships can be career changing.

Get Engaged Followers

You can't simply ask someone to be a superfan. Creating authentic sponsorship starts with one simple requirement: your work must speak positively for you. You must do good work. Period. Full stop. You won't get a fan—much less a superfan—if you don't provide value to the company. Leaders won't risk sponsoring you if your performance isn't consistently good. You must deliver—no exceptions. Delivering consistently good work and adding value becomes part of how you are recognized—your personal brand. It positions you as a unique talent.

To get your engaged followers, don't look for just anyone with power to be your sponsor. Look for sponsorship grounded in authenticity, which requires an investment. In an authentic sponsorship relationship, you arm your sponsor with the information they need to be knowledgeable about your skills and goals. They then have specific details about you and are able to demonstrate pride in your performance while using their voice to tell your story. You transform them from sponsor to superfan by establishing a relationship grounded on clarity, completeness, and connection.

First, find clarity. Think about what you want and how a sponsor will help you. Be clear about why you need sponsorship. What do you need this specific sponsor for? What do you want to achieve? Are you aiming for a promotion? An expanded role? A growth position in a different area? These are all things to consider as you set your future course.

Once your direction is set, it's important to provide potential sponsors with your complete story. Be vulnerable and share more than just your work history. It's tempting to keep your sponsorship request to just business—the next opportunity or project you seek or your skills and experiences. But advocacy is so much stronger when sponsors know you as more than just facts and accomplishments.

When a sponsor understands your bigger goals, your unique talents, what motivates you, what excites you, and why the next opportunity matters to you, you've started to create a connected, authentic superfan. Share your personal story, your ambitions, and what sets you apart from other individuals. Let your sponsor get to know you on a more complete level. Use the sponsorship opportunity to communicate your unique, personal brand. Explain how this influences your leadership style and impacts the contributions you make to the company. Your sponsor should be able to tell others the unique value that they will get when they hire you.

Once the superfan connection is made, stay connected. Reach out to your sponsor with regular updates and for quick discussions. Let your sponsor know what is going well and what is challenging. Keep them informed about your goals, especially if anything changes for you. It's important that your sponsor has the latest information about you and your career goals. You never know when an opportunity that's right for you will present itself to your sponsor, and you don't want a lack of knowledge to be a barrier. Give them the information to rave all about you!

Why is it so important to bring clarity, completeness, and connection to the sponsorship relationship? You can enlist sponsors without these three components, and many sponsors only look for strong job performance and the ability to add value. However, when you are a woman or a minority woman, you want to be valued and sponsored for the unique contributions you make. You want to advance by demonstrating your authentic leadership style and unique talents. The goal is not to be viewed as just another rising star but to be viewed as a one-of-a-kind star. Authentic sponsorship can help achieve this star status by creating followers who recognize your talents and contributions as well as who you are.

Authenticity in Action

The true value of a sponsor is found in how well they advocate for you. This can be done informally when your sponsor talks with peers after a meeting or formally during talent discussions and the job vetting process.

When it comes to talent and succession meetings, I always come extra prepared. We're often discussing up-and-coming talent with leadership potential—specifically, the individuals we think will advance to senior leadership roles—so these meetings can be difficult. Leaders advocate for their star talent and wait to see if they are challenged or if there is agreement in the room.

One meeting began with a discussion of Ms. P, a talented African American woman whose story I knew very well. A colleague kicked off the discussion by saying, "I've been impressed with her this year. She has expanded her leadership responsibilities and successfully managed a tough client group. I think in a year's time, Ms. P could be a vice president sitting at this table."

Before I could add my endorsement, another colleague, a longtime leader in the organization, added rich details and examples describing Ms. P's goals and ambitions.

I smiled to myself as I observed the level of sponsorship coming from the two leaders. I added my comments, agreeing with both of my colleagues, and offered some additional insight into her work with her team and commitment to growth and development.

As the meeting closed, I reflected on my coaching relationship with Ms. P. She knew I was her follower and superfan. We had discussed the importance of developing sponsors who are strong followers and how this was especially true for women of color. But what impressed me was that she had done the work to create a group of superfans who knew her work and her interests. There were at least three of us who were superfan followers! Job well done, Ms. P! Ms. P was promoted to vice president.

Hidden Gems: Secret Sponsorship

While it's important to seek authentic sponsors and followers who can help you achieve your career goals, we often unknowingly create followers.

As a woman or minority woman leader, you will likely be more visible than your counterparts because of your gender, race, or ethnicity. You may be the only woman or only minority involved in certain projects or the only one serving as a leader or member of a team. The combination of your unique talents and skills, as well as your perspective as a woman or minority, makes you valuable and makes you stand out.

Leaders who take their talent development responsibilities seriously are always observing and on the lookout for up-and-coming talent. They want talent they can sponsor when the right opportunity presents itself. Your work will speak for itself, and when it speaks positively for you, others whom you may not even have identified as a sponsor may see your unique talent.

Bottom line? No one has the same combination of traits, experiences, skills, and capabilities as you. Your unique talents should be embraced and not hidden. It's important that you own and protect your distinctive brand by always doing good work and letting your uniqueness shine. This way, when a secret sponsor—one you didn't select but who selected you—has an opportunity to advocate for you, there will be no hesitancy on their part, and the brand they communicate will be your authentic brand.

Remember: your work and your actions create your brand. Take authentic ownership of both!

Actively developing sponsorship is an essential part of becoming a strong leader in a corporate environment. You must seek sponsorship for yourself, no matter your level. And you must provide it to others. As a leader, one of your greatest commitments is to develop talent. Sponsorship helps you fulfill that commitment. But do more. Seek authentic sponsorship for yourself and provide authentic sponsorship for others.

Your authenticity is your currency, and your ability to see the authenticity of others will set you apart as a leader. Take the opportunity to encourage followers and likes. If you embrace your authenticity and do good work, don't be surprised when your followers turn into superfans.

Authenticity Lessons & Reflections

1. **Seeking a sponsor is critical for career development, but you must be clear about your authentic brand.** *What sets you apart from others? What are your unique skills and talents? How do those skills and talents combine with your lived experience to create your authentic brand?*

2. **Sponsors are different than mentors. They help expand your value and leverage your brand by letting others know about your authentic value.** *Who are your sponsors? Why have you selected them? Are you engaging in authentic sponsorship with clarity, completeness, and connection? What can you improve upon?*

3. **Good leaders follow unique and diverse talent.** *Whose talents do you follow? How are these individuals similar to you? How can you help individuals who bring a unique and authentic brand to their work? How can you bring greater diversity to your sponsorship?*

CHAPTER 9

CHANGE BREEDS OPPORTUNITY

I've weathered many changes. Some were great, and some weren't, but I learned one important thing—change breeds opportunity! This actually became my mantra, and I must have said it at least a thousand times during the last decade of my corporate career. But saying it and understanding it are two separate things. It takes commitment and perseverance to transform change into opportunity.

When you're in the corporate world, change is inevitable. It's a part of life. How you respond to change defines who you are and where you're headed. That doesn't mean you have to like change, but you have to understand that how you respond to change is important. Ultimately, you have to look beyond the difficult or scary parts of change to find new opportunities.

True leaders develop skill sets that help them thrive during change. They learn to embrace the discomfort because they know there is a lot of potential to be found on the other side.

Refocus

As a corporate leader, I often found myself coaching people about how to handle impending changes to their team, role, or responsibilities. Sometimes, it was working with a mentee who was seeking to redirect her career and create a new opportunity for herself. Other times, it involved working with a team to integrate a process or policy change that meant doing things differently.

No matter what the actual change was, one thing was consistent. The person or team going through the change suddenly had myopia! They could only see loss. Their perspective became clouded by the overwhelming feeling of something being done to them—a loss of control. The person may have hated their role and longed for organizational change. Or her career may have stagnated, and she had the skill set to create a new one. Or maybe, she was constantly struggling with a ridiculous process and had a ton of ideas that would improve workflow. No matter how much the current situation hurt, the change was viewed narrow-mindedly and seen as much more painful than the status quo.

The pain of change can make us feel victimized by the environment or the situation over which we feel we have no control. During these moments, it's normal to feel less valued, especially when our focus shifts back rather than forward. When we focus on holding onto the old, we can become disheartened with the change and question our ability to survive, much less thrive, in the new. Sometimes we even disconnect from what we know to be true, which is our own authentic value. We may lose our bearings and forget the unique qualities and capabilities that we bring to every situation. When we anchor ourselves to the old and shun the new, we risk becoming a victim of change.

What I know to be true is that we bring skills, talents, and experiences to our work that cannot be replicated by anyone else.

When we embrace this authentic, universal truth about ourselves, change can breed opportunity.

I learned this the hard way during a career change that challenged my leadership and forced me to refocus, face my fears, facilitate, and fine-tune in order to create a new opportunity.

I was sitting in my office around 10:00 a.m. when my phone rang. A quick glance at the screen told me I should answer the call. It was my boss.

She got right to the point, "Ms. L is restructuring her organization and will have a couple of roles that would be good for you. You've done a great job leading our migration, and she'd like to speak with you if you're interested."

"I am definitely interested," I stated. I was more than a little stressed about what was next for me. I had taken a position leading a two-year migration project, knowing I'd need to find a new role once the project ended, which was very soon.

I had applied for the role that excited me, and my interview went well. I anxiously awaited a call from the vice president.

Late Friday afternoon, the call finally came. After a few pleasantries, Ms. L delivered the news. "I'd like to offer you the director position that leads our project management office, service quality, and auditing!" she said excitedly.

Slap in the face! This was not the role I had applied for, and it interested me the very least. I hadn't even considered it. To top it off, the salary came in below my expectations. I gave my salary expectations along with my rationale to Ms. L, and she met my salary request.

I had a new job, but I wasn't excited about it. I would stay for two years, I told myself. That would be long enough to make an impact, gain visibility with senior management, and perfect some new skills.

Note to all authentic women: never take a position you're not excited about! I hated my new role! Hated it.

While I was learning some new skills, most of my time was spent doing things that did not excite me. But the fun didn't end there. I had joined a team that had been together for quite some time, and the environment was toxic. There were alliances and cliques, yet each person seemed to work alone and for their own benefit. Early on, I had many sit-down meetings with different peers to address aggressive behaviors directed towards me that I would not tolerate. Within three months, I was literally counting down the days till my personal two-year commitment was fulfilled.

I had survived for almost a year when budget time arrived. We had an aggressive target to meet, and Ms. L challenged us to rethink our organization's structure, including our own roles. True to the team's dysfunctional form, we parted ways and developed our plans separately.

This exercise scared me to death! I had to consider the possibility of eliminating my own role. I was working this out alone and realized that I might be putting myself back on the path to finding a new job. Did I want that?

When examining the different options, I quickly realized that the best plan would be to combine two of our groups under a single leader—merging my PMO team with the project management team. This created efficiencies and saved money by eliminating a leadership role. I would not be the leader for the combined organization because I did not want the role. This plan would sacrifice me for what was best for the organization, and at that moment, I simply couldn't do it.

My change myopia had kicked in, and I was looking backward, not forward. I rationalized my choice by saying, "The devil you do know is better than the one you don't." I could make a case for keeping the two teams separate. Let them find the money elsewhere!

When we presented our recommendations, I argued insincerely and inauthentically that my organization needed to remain separate for objectivity. I could see that no one on the team, including our leader, agreed. Ultimately, someone broke the silence and addressed the elephant in the room. "What if we put the project management and the PMO teams together under a single leader?" they asked.

There, it was out. Exhale. The moment I heard the suggestion, I was relieved. This was an opportunity to own my fate and get out of a role I absolutely abhorred. I would be back in the unknown again, a fearful place, but once the idea was on the table, I knew I could let go of my current role and focus on creating a new future.

In my fear, I had lost an important connection with myself. I had forgotten my inherent value and what made me unique. I had forgotten that I've found jobs before, and I would do it again. I had the skills and talents I came into the role with plus new experiences and skills to add to my resume. I could do this.

"I agree with that idea," I said. "I think that she would be great at managing the combined organization." I looked at my peer to my right who managed the project managers and smiled genuinely, authentically. I meant it.

Reframe Change

I may be dating myself a little, but have you ever gone to the circus and watched acrobats high above your head do a trapeze act? There's always that moment when the acrobat flies from one swinging trapeze to another. The crowd gasps during the nanosecond when the acrobat is freefalling in midair, after letting go of the first trapeze and before grabbing the second one.

That period of freefall is experienced when we go through change. It's the gap between the old and the new. It's the space where you can decide how much pain you experience and how quickly you navigate the change.

Traditional change models don't address this gap or moment of letting go. Most simply describe a process of initial resistance, letting go of the old, then accepting the new. The process is fairly consistent, but it's in the space between the old and new where true change happens. During the freefall moment is where you can accelerate the change process and minimize the pain. By tapping into your authenticity and remembering what makes you unique and valuable, you can more effectively reframe the change experience.

Incorporating change into your life and reframing career changes can be done by implementing the four Fs—find your fear, facilitate, focus, and fine-tune.

Find Your FEAR

When change comes along, we often feel afraid. Be clear about what you're afraid of and where it comes from. Then, move toward the fear. You heard me: **move toward fear**. That which makes us uncomfortable makes us grow. Feel the fear and do it anyway. That's called courage. Creating an authentic career requires courage.

FACILITATE Don't Fight

Don't fight change that you cannot control. Become a facilitator. Influence and affect the change you would like to see happen. Do not allow yourself to become a victim of the change. Take an active role in facilitating outcomes. When you become a facilitator, you are actually regaining a modicum of control that you can build from to define your new future.

FOCUS on the Bigger Picture

As a leader, we must look at organizational change from the perspective of how it impacts our team and the organization—first and foremost. It's always about others first when you are a leader. There is no room for selfishness in leadership.

There are also personal advantages to focusing on the bigger picture. Think about how organizational change can benefit you. What is changing? What new opportunities or possibilities does this create for you? If you no longer have your current responsibilities, what could you pursue or create for yourself?

FINE-TUNE Your Value

This is the foundational principle for reframing change. Remember your value. As I've said before, your experience, knowledge, skills, and talents cannot be taken from you. Together, with all your other qualities, you are a unique individual who is inherently valuable. When change comes along, it's important to reconnect with what makes us valuable, assess what opportunities the change creates, and fine-tune what we have to offer. Fine-tuning means we compare what we have to offer with the environment created by the change. We then tune into how our uniqueness can bring value to the new environment.

Reframe Change

If I had focused on the four Fs, I might have been better prepared to face a change that I really needed. But I was so afraid of not having a role that I was willing to fight to keep a role I hated. I knew the right answer, but I chose to ignore it because, at the time, I lacked the courage. I had been myopic, only seeing my loss.

My solid business thought processes were overshadowed by a selfishness driven by fear. When you are given the privilege to lead others and to make decisions that impact their daily lives, you must put them first by focusing on the bigger picture.

Once I accepted that change was inevitable, I moved into a facilitator role—advocating for the combined organization and supporting the transition to my peer. I was then able to tune into organizational changes and see more clearly what I had to offer. I ended up finding a bigger role in another division. The position included more of the functions I enjoyed and greater responsibility. Change breeds opportunity.

Authenticity in Action

When we're most unsure of a change is when we need to focus on the four Fs and use our authenticity to create opportunity. This was the case with Ms. D, a talented young mentee of mine.

My phone buzzed with a text message from Ms. D. "Hey!" the message read. "You are talking to a newly promoted staff vice president!"

"OMG! Congratulations!" I texted back, scheduling a time to catch up and celebrate.

When we had met, Ms. D was a shy, intelligent, motivated individual contributor who had the ambition and ability to do more. She wanted to get into management, and we worked together to make her dream a reality. My coaching role was to keep her grounded in her authenticity and to provide insights to help her overcome barriers.

She put in the work, and in no time, she was managing her first team. In another year or so, she was managing other managers. Now, a short time later, she was promoted again. But the journey to this promotion had been rooted in change that was beyond her control.

I remember a "change" conversation we had just a few months before her latest promotion. She was a little distressed. "You're not going to believe what happened! My boss was fired," she explained in disbelief. "As of two weeks ago, I report to the senior vice president."

"Wow. That's a big change," I had said. "Lots of things can happen when new leaders come in."

"Yeah. I can tell there will be some challenges there. Just the way things are going on a couple of key priorities, it seems like the new guy is not easy to work with," she explained.

"So, tell me what you're afraid of," I replied.

"He doesn't know me. My old manager hired me and knew what I could do. He was my sponsor and supported the direction I was taking with this team. Now, I work for a leader who is super busy. We had one brief one-on-one where we didn't really dive much into what I do. We communicate mostly via email. He's running crazy right now," she said.

"So clearly, he's new and drinking from the firehose," I said. "What do you think he needs right now in this moment?"

"Support. Someone who knows how things work. A strategic perspective. Everything to keep running smoothly," she answered.

"How can you help with those things? How can you be of value during this change? What skills do you bring to the table that you can really draw on to help?" I asked.

"Well, I have responsibility for the operations and some key strategic projects. I could make sure that things run smoothly, keep him up to date proactively, educate him as much as I can," she said.

"Mmm-hmm," I said. "I'm guessing, right now, with the firing of your manager, he lost a consolidator. Your boss had responsibility for many functions, which you know about. You have a strong strategic perspective, and you're an executor. You have a way of telling the difficult truth to people so that it can be heard and acted upon. Might your new boss need that?" I was being sarcastic with the last comment.

"You're right. I think I could be of help," she said.

"Focus on the big picture—not just you—and on how you can add value. Fine-tune what you bring to the table that is helpful in this moment. Stepping up to report to a senior vice president is huge for you. This is a career moment. Embrace it. You never know where it could go. Don't fight it," I advised. We went on to discuss what it's like to report to a senior vice president and how now was not the time to be selfish and focus solely on herself. Instead, she could be the bridge—the facilitator—between her new leader and the organization.

Ms. D did just that and demonstrated her value. In a few months, she was rewarded with a well-deserved promotion, the third in almost as many years.

Change is the name of the game when you're in leadership in corporate America and, honestly, in life. As humans, it's not easy to change, but we can certainly make the change journey quicker and less painful. Your authenticity is your rudder. Let it guide and stabilize you through the ups and downs of your change journey. Remember, your value cannot be changed or destroyed because it is as unique as your fingerprint. You carry it with you always. It's always evolving. Move toward the fear. Facilitate. Focus. Fine-tune. Create your future. You've got this, girl!

Authenticity Lessons & Reflections

1. **There is value in the freefall from old to new. Find it.** *What changes are you resisting in your life? What is your greatest fear? What steps can you take to move toward that fear?*

2. **Don't be a victim by letting environmental or situational factors influence your perception of your value.** *What situations or beliefs have caused you to think less of or to forget your unique value? What is the truth about your value? How has your value expanded in your current environment?*

3. **Fear is a fair reaction to change, but as a leader, you cannot allow fear to create selfishness.** *There is no room for selfishness in leadership. When has selfishness impacted your leadership? What is the bigger picture that you must focus upon? How do you add value to the bigger picture?*

CHAPTER 10

WHY?

As women leaders, we sometimes get so busy with the business of life and work that we lose sight of our bigger purpose—the "why" behind everything we do. When we're comfortable and in the flow of life, our purpose, or what drives us to create an authentic career, seems to matter less. Things are going smoothly, so it's easy to just move along. Eventually, though, we may become lost or disconnected from what inspires us and gives us purpose.

When we lose our way, it's never too late to find our purpose again and create the authentic career we love. Sometimes it's a matter of making a small change to our current role. Other times, we may completely shift our perspective or job, changing to a new industry, specialty, or even profession. While the journey to finding or reconnecting with your purpose and making it happen can be full of challenges, the benefits of a purpose-driven career are far greater than the few bumps along the way.

Creating an Authentic Career

The distinction between having a career and having an authentic career is purpose. An authentic career is created when your unique skills, talents, and experiences connect to your purpose, which is what defines the underlying "why" for what you do with your career.

Your purpose is something you absolutely must do. It is magnetic, attractive, compelling, and hard to ignore—like a candle flame that draws a moth ever closer. While your purpose may change at different stages in your life, it always remains your "why" and compels you to create an authentic career each time it shifts.

My journey to an authentic career began when I was thirty-nine years old and pregnant with our youngest child. I was a regional vice president responsible for a multifunction organization spanning five states with almost 300 employees. I was just a step below the executive ranks. Every day, I woke up at 6:00 a.m., packed my older two kids off to school and daycare, and then led a 7:30 a.m. call on operational improvement with my boss and peers as I drove to the office.

I did this every morning, worked a full eight to nine hours in the office, returned home to spend the evening with my family, slept, and did it again. I was in this cyclic routine when, at eight months pregnant, I heard the tiniest voice in my head whisper to me: "How did you get here?"

After our daughter was born, the voice was shouting, "How did you get here!" and I could no longer ignore it. I pondered the answer for twelve weeks while on maternity leave. I had come to my company for tuition reimbursement almost twenty years earlier, and now, I was in a job that I couldn't say I loved. I had gotten there through hard work, education, a desire to achieve, and a willingness to take on tough challenges. I had benefitted financially, for sure, and I was grateful. I knew my job mattered, but I was working almost fifty hours a week doing something I did not love.

The truth was my career was driven by the next challenge rather than an overarching purpose. Tuition reimbursement had brought me to the company, but exciting challenges had kept me there. I rode the wave of whatever new challenge came my way. Many times, others sought me out to clarify complicated projects. Other times, I sought specific, demanding projects. I was always asking myself, "What more am I capable of doing?" But rarely, if ever, did I ask myself, "Why do I want to do this work? What is my purpose?"

At the end of my maternity leave, I knew one thing—I had failed to own my career. I chose every single job and challenge, but I had not created an authentic career that I loved.

Find Your Purpose

How do you begin to find your purpose and create an authentic career? There are three basic tenets that will help you navigate the change—listen to the dissonance, find your why, and persevere.

Listen to the Dissonance

Dissonance is the noise created when there is a disconnect between who you are and who you want to be. Simply put, it means you are in disagreement with yourself. The disagreement may be about a specific role, your career trajectory, your work-life balance, or anything else that consistently bothers you. No matter how specific or how expansive, the disagreement creates internal noise. It's the sound of you resisting yourself, resisting what is true for you.

What does that noise sound like? Sometimes it's a tiny voice telling you that you could do better, or you could do more. Sometimes, it's not even a voice: it's an experience or an emotion. It's feeling invisible when you know your contributions are making a difference. It's feeling tolerated and not appreciated for the value you bring. It's a feeling that's holding you back from participating in a meeting for fear that what you have to say will be ignored or stolen from you by someone else in the room. That noise represents a painful sentiment—this is not me.

Women and minority women get good at ignoring that noise. Why don't we listen? One reason is that the fight for a successful career is so challenging for women and minorities that listening to a voice telling us to head in a different direction, especially after we've achieved a level of success, may feel asinine. It also takes courage to listen to that internal voice telling you to step away from what you know and are comfortable with.

Making a purpose-driven change can be tough. For women, it often means putting ourselves first and following our own path. That feels selfish. We're the caregivers. We put others first. For minority women, following the voice inside could mean stepping away from a sure thing or starting the career climb all over again. Who knows if you'll be able to find another job that pays as well, offers such great benefits, or is this close to the top of the house?

Building an authentic career where you are connected to your unique purpose requires that you listen to the dissonance. Don't fear it. Listen closely to it. You may not know what the next step is, but the dissonance is the alarm. Like a fire alarm, never ignore it! Your purpose will be your guide.

Find Your Why

With the dissonance alarm going off, it's time to consider your why. Authentic careers are tied to purpose and answer the question—why does this work matter to me? Determining the answer requires that you think through your values and the impact you want to have through your work. Notice, I didn't say it requires that you know exactly what role or job you want to do. You first need to focus on what you value and the impact you want to have.

I've found the best way to find your "why" is to work from two different perspectives: self-reflection and feedback from others.

Self-Reflection

Self-reflection involves setting aside time so that you can determine your values and the impact you want to have with your career. It takes dedicated, quiet, and uninterrupted time to be self-reflective. I suggest having something to capture your thoughts. Take notes.

Here are the steps.

1. Identify your passions, interests, and the things that bring you joy—personally and professionally. No limits.
2. Identify your skills, talents, expertise, and unique-lived experiences.
3. Identify your core values. These are the things that mean the most to you, and anything you do (personally or professionally) must uphold them.
4. Think through times when you were in the zone while working, volunteering, or doing something personally meaningful. What were you doing when in that zone where you lost track of time and experienced joy? Take specific note of what you

were doing, why you enjoyed it, and the skills, talents, or expertise you were using.

5.   Complete this sentence: I am in the zone when _____ _____.

Feedback from Others

Objective, honest feedback is an important part of finding your why. We rarely see what others see, and many times we underestimate our capabilities and impact. Reach out to truth-tellers, casual mentors, sponsors, friends, family, people who work for you, people you work with, people you know from volunteer work, and/or anyone in your network who has a perspective that you trust and value. Ask at least five people who will offer you different perspectives.

Ask these questions and take notes.

1.   What do you see as my strengths? What do I excel at?
2.   What seems to put me in the zone? What seems to energize me?
3.   What seems to zap my energy?
4.   When you think of me, what can you picture me doing well as a career?

Now, combine your self-reflection and feedback to complete the following questions:

I can use my unique skills, talents, expertise, and experiences to _____.
(List as many things as you like.)

I want to use my career to _____.
(List the ways you want to have an impact.)

My career purpose or "why" is_____.
(Identify the one thing you feel most drawn to do.)

Answering these questions is a starting point and will help you identify where to focus your efforts on your next career opportunity. Once you know the unique value you bring to your career and the impact you want to have, you are well on your way to finding roles that help you achieve your objective.

Persevere

Having an authentic career requires courage. The courage to hear what dissonance is telling you. The courage to find your purpose. And the courage to fight for what your purpose says you must do. When in doubt about the choices you are making to create your authentic career, turn back to your purpose and values. Look at the impact you want to have and stay focused.

Here are some tips to help you persevere when doubt and insecurity creep in.

Tip #1: Keep your focus on the bigger journey. Always remember how your current career choice or the changes you're making fit into the bigger picture. Think about how they align with the impact you want to have and your purpose.

Tip #2: Share your career purpose with those who support you—spouses, partners, friends, truth-tellers, sponsors. They will be your cheerleaders during the difficult times, keeping you grounded in your truth if you stray from your purpose.

Tip #3: Be willing to make creative adjustments and to work for what you want. You may have to educate yourself, supplement your income, or modify your approach to ultimately realize your career purpose. Adjustments are fine when they help you stay on the path to your purpose.

I took these tips to heart. After self-reflection and feedback, I began networking and interviewing and found a purpose-driven role in human resources as a program director leading talent management initiatives. To some, it was a shameful demotion. The position was several rungs down the corporate ladder. To me, I had just taken two tiny steps back to make a huge leap forward. For what felt like the first time, my purpose and my work made sense. I was completely satisfied with my career choice because I completely owned it.

The journey still had challenges, and I learned to persevere. Following my purpose wasn't paying all the bills. We were struggling financially and trying to determine how we'd make ends meet. We had two mortgages: our home in Cincinnati and the one we lived in. My family was also adjusting to the move to a new city, so I changed my work schedule to work from home three days a week.

My salary stayed the same in my new role, but because my old role paid more than the new program director role, I would get no raises, and my bonus was significantly reduced. Anthony got a job. And realizing that this was a season and not a lifetime, I reduced my contributions to my 401K, the kids' college fund, our Christmas account, and our emergency savings.

The financial changes helped, along with Anthony's paycheck from his part-time work at the local grocery store. I stayed focused on my purpose as I studied for and passed my HR Certification exams. I wanted to accelerate my learning curve so that I could better contribute to the organization. My continued development paid off, and I moved quickly from a program director role to a leadership role to a business partner role.

The business partner role was where the rubber hit the road in human resources. I coordinated all human resource needs for a senior leadership team and their executive leader. It was a difficult job for me. I was expected to be extremely knowledgeable about all human resource matters, and I was still learning.

One day, I got a call from one of the leaders I supported. She asked me to stop by her office to talk. It was strange to hear from her, and I had an uneasy feeling. After some brief chitchat, she started on the reason for her call.

"Several of the leaders have come to me talking about you. They feel that you aren't engaged enough with our team. Since you work at home three days a week, they feel you are not able to take advantage of being here together in this building. They would like to see you more involved in their staff meetings and more proactive on the things they need." She took a deep breath and detailed specific examples when the leaders felt I had not done enough or was not sufficiently knowledgeable or proactive.

Gut punch. Stinging of tears behind my eyes. If they only knew how hard this job was for me. It required a higher level of engagement and interaction than I had ever had in my career, and my training had been limited at best. I was doing my best as I was learning, and clearly, that wasn't good enough. My work-at-home schedule had been to help my family adjust to our relocation. I was doing my best to meet everyone's needs, or so I thought. This is so often the dilemma for women. It's so ironic that working at home was ever an issue when now, it's much more the norm.

"Thank you," I managed to say. "I can't address what I don't know about. I will think about what you said and let you know what my plan is. I appreciate you telling me." I stood to leave. She could see that I was hurt.

When I got home that evening, I cried with Anthony by my side. He asked, "So, what's the plan?"

"I brought us here to help me live my purpose. No one said it would be easy. This is just part of the journey," I said. Anthony understood how this role fit with my purpose, and we agreed that I would go back to working full time in the office and focus on learning my role better.

I worked hard, and in a few years, I went on to a senior role in the human resources department, leading the largest group of human resource business partners in the organization. I brought all my experience, skills, and talents to the role. My voice was now amplified by the team I had the privilege to lead.

Authenticity in Action

Sometimes we need an outside perspective to help us connect to our purpose. Remember Ms. D, the woman who created opportunity out of the change of losing her manager and reporting to a new senior vice president? Her journey to success started with finding her "why." When she found her purpose, it transformed her career.

When I met Ms. D, she was different from the woman she became. The seeds were there: she was intelligent, motivated, ambitious, and capable. But the flower couldn't bloom because Ms. D was invisible. Her work was strong, and her manager knew it. The work was shared higher in the organization, and the organization benefitted, but Ms. D didn't get the visibility.

She was the workhorse behind the scenes. Conversations with her manager about career development didn't yield results. And when Ms. D spoke with other, more tenured Black employees in the department, she was saddened to learn that their experiences were like hers, and they had no hope of things ever changing. She was defeated when she showed up at my office.

"I just feel like I'm running in mud," Ms. D shared. She had just told me about the great work she was doing and how her many attempts to engage her manager in a conversation about career development had failed.

"Where do you want to go next with your career? Do you know?" I asked.

"I'm not exactly sure. I just know I can do more," she replied.

"Being able to do more is great, but what's your real purpose? What do you feel driven to do?" I asked.

Ms. D didn't have a clear answer for that. She was so focused on getting away from her current role that she hadn't really thought much about what she was moving toward.

Through our conversations, she decided to get involved in our company's employee resource groups and to take a lead role in driving key initiatives. I connected her with leaders who could serve as mentors and sponsors so she could start networking to become more visible and to discover what interested her most.

A few months went by, and Ms. D was in my office for another meeting. I had a job opening, and she was interested in the role.

"I'd like to come work for you," Ms. D explained.

We discussed the requirements for the role, and although the role wasn't a perfect fit, I had no doubt that she could learn the job. It would be a steep learning curve, but this young woman was smart. The real challenge was that she was still running away from her current role and not toward her purpose.

"Honestly, I don't think this role is the best fit for you. With time, you could absolutely do it, but you still need to find your purpose. What are you really excited about doing? I've heard you talk about managing people. Why? You have to figure that out and find a role that will give you the opportunity to do what you love," I explained. She agreed that the open role wasn't for her, but she was frustrated and felt stuck.

"Patience and perseverance," I told her. "Keep doing great work. Use the resource group and your network to figure out what you really want."

"I don't want to bother people with my search for the right role. It feels like I'm just using them," Ms. D said.

"Networking is an exchange. It's not a one-way street. What if you have something they can learn from you? No one has cornered the market on talent. No one is like you, and you have something to offer just like anyone else, below your level or above," I told her.

Over the next few months, Ms. D took an active role in the resource group, leading them through several impactful projects and initiatives. She stepped into a state-level leadership role with the group and continued networking. She took copious notes and made the most of her time with each person.

In our next coaching session, Ms. D shared that she had applied for a manager position. As we prepared for her interview, Ms. D described how her resource group work had helped her discover how much she loves leading, sharing, and helping others. Ms. D certainly had the expertise for the role she was applying for, and she also had a passion for leading people. It was no surprise that she got the job!

We continued our coaching relationship, focusing our conversations on how to lead authentically because getting the job was easier than maintaining it. In her manager role, Ms. D encountered team members who were older and more tenured than she was. It was tempting to succumb to the pressure to be accepted and not to challenge current processes or not chart a new path for the team. But Ms. D was passionate about leading people. She stayed motivated by keeping her bigger picture in mind and focused on how her leadership could bring people together to accomplish common goals.

Ms. D sat down in my office. As a first-time, new manager, she was facing blatant disregard for her direction and disrespect that approached insubordination from some team members.

"How would you describe your leadership style?" I asked.

"I'm direct, approachable, supportive, and I have high expectations for myself and those who work with me," she rattled off effortlessly. She knew who she was.

"I know about your challenges, but what has been the overall reaction to you as the new manager? What feedback are you getting?" I asked.

"My director says I'm doing a great job. He keeps giving me support and letting me take the lead to make changes. The changes are working. Our numbers look much better. Many of the people who report to me have told me they like what I'm doing. It's just two individuals who are clearly not on board," she explained thoughtfully.

Ms. D went on to explain that the individuals were struggling with the changes she was making, and she felt she should adjust to make them more comfortable.

"Maybe I should give them more time to get on board? I don't know. But seems like, as the leader, it's on me to make it work," she said almost as a question.

"I think you have a responsibility for the success of your team, but you don't have responsibility for the behaviors of those who choose not to be led," I shared. We discussed how she was quite different from what they have experienced in a leader. She was a direct, supportive African American woman who was younger and with a different lived experience professionally and personally. That made it difficult for the two to accept Ms. D's leadership.

I advised her, "If you are respectful and just as supportive of the two who are not on board as you are of the others, you'll be fine. Smile like you always do and be you. They will adjust or make their own decisions about what they want to do with their careers. Stay true to your leadership."

Ms. D continued to grow in her leadership, delivering great results. Clearly living her purpose, she attracted many young women who came to her for career advice, and she always made time for them, challenging them to take actions that would help them grow and achieve their career goals.

We continued our coaching conversations over the course of the year when she pursued another higher role with greater responsibility. This position was a big step in her career, and she successfully obtained it, beating out other candidates who had deeper subject matter expertise. Why? Because her authentic leadership, driven by her purpose to lead, share, and help others, got results. She was in her zone, doing what she must do, and the results spoke for themselves.

Careers can be cobbled together from unrelated roles and experiences, or they can be a set of clear steps heading up the corporate ladder. Regardless of the career path followed, it is most meaningful when you own it—when it becomes your authentic career driven by your purpose. You'll know when the authenticity is missing. The question is, how will you respond?

Authenticity Lessons & Reflections

1. **Dissonance sounds the alarm. Never ignore it.** *What causes dissonance between your work and who you are? What does it sound and look like? How can you close the gap?*

2. **Purpose grounds us and serves as a filter to run our choices through.** *What is your purpose? How can you connect your purpose to your current role? What would make your work experiences more aligned with your purpose? Is there a different work choice that you could make to align better with your purpose?*

3. **Having a strong purpose doesn't guarantee the work will be easy. You must persevere to create an authentic career that you love.** *What are the challenges to creating the authentic career you love? Who in your network can help you? What other resources do you need?*

CHAPTER 11

PUT YOUR VOICE
IN THE ROOM

The most common way that people give up their power is by thinking they don't have any.

—Alice Walker

Stereotypes about what women can and should do or say abound, especially for women of color. In the corporate world, women balance a unique set of demands, challenges, and expectations. We want to be respected and valued for our contributions, but we simultaneously have to spend time and energy positioning our points of view so that they will be received well by the majority. Speaking your truth can get you labeled as pushy, too direct, angry, aggressive, or a bitch.

How do we balance these conflicting demands? You find your authentic voice and use it. What you have to offer is unique and can make an impact. Regardless of the time or the place, speaking up and using your voice is never a poor choice. In fact, it can make all the difference.

Finding Your Authentic Voice

No one shares your DNA. No one is like you. No one in the world has your exact combination of skills, talents, and life experiences. You are unique, and so is your voice. When you are given an opportunity to lead or have an impact, you must be responsible and accountable. Your voice matters, and when you don't use it, you lose power and authenticity.

Finding your authentic voice is easy. It's the voice you can own and stick by, regardless of the outcome. And using your voice is not simply about being heard. It's about what you have to say. Always put your voice in the room as a beacon of value. When you deny yourself the opportunity to add value, you inherently devalue yourself.

This doesn't mean speaking up to repeat what others say for the sake of being heard. It means speaking up to add value or insight. Holding back your value or insight when you know it could be meaningful and have an impact does not serve or honor you. It makes you feel inauthentic.

I experienced one of the challenges of sharing your voice after just beginning a new job as the human resources business partner for a senior leadership team. I was on my third call with the team, and they were discussing a job candidate who had just completed a final interview. We were discussing a critical open position for the team where having someone effective would be a game-changer.

After completing the final two interviews and reviewing our assessments, it was clear that none of the candidates had the skills necessary to elevate the role and meet the executive leader's needs.

"Our interim leader has done a good job holding things together," one of the leaders shared. "I guess we should just stay with her." Other team members agreed, citing the length of the process and the need to satisfy their manager.

My mind raced as I listened to the conversation. None of these candidates were who they needed. My stomach rolled a little as I thought about that. Several weeks had been spent on the selection process. The team was weary, and their manager was frustrated. He had been clear that this needed to get done as soon as possible.

I had joined as the final phase of the selection process had begun. As the newbie on the team, I didn't know most of them, and they didn't know me. They certainly didn't know my style. I could be direct, and I knew it, but directness always seemed to go down better when you had some type of relationship with the person you were being direct with.

Although no one on this team knew me, I knew something had to be done because this team was about to make a mistake. They were settling, and I needed to call them on their bullshit right now. How do I tell them? How would they feel about me raising the bar? Would they respect the newbie's perspective or just try to override me?

The scales of justice appeared in my mind. Speak up and risk insulting or alienating some of the team members or go along with a recommendation that I didn't agree with for the sake of expediency and getting the boss off all our backs.

Not finding the best candidate certainly wasn't my fault. Was it worth offering a different point of view? And, if I offered my perspective, what next? Start the process over? Would I be viewed as a roadblock? A problem-maker? Or would my voice be valued?

Maybe, we could find the best person for the role, and the organization would be better for it. But I just wanted to be thought of as beneficial and an important, valuable member of the team. It was clear that meeting their manager's expectations and avoiding conflict was what they valued, and I was considering going against both those values. I was not sure where that would leave me with this group.

This nagging voice inside me spoke, "If you don't say something, you're not being true to yourself, and you're certainly not offering the benefit of your knowledge and expertise. If you don't speak up, you're saying their perspective is more valuable than yours. After you do that once, when do you stop? How do you find your voice after you ignore it? You are here for a reason—to add value. If they shoot you down, so be it. At least you spoke up. If they don't shoot you down, you have an opportunity to make a difference in with this role."

I spoke up.

"This is a critical role, and you've all indicated that none of the candidates has what is needed. So, we keep looking," I said. The team accepted my suggestion after some more discussion but left me on my own to deliver the news to their manager.

I made the difficult call to a very frustrated and irate executive leader later that evening. My stomach flipped again as I pressed him on how well he felt the interim candidate met his unique expectations for the role. He paused before he replied, "You've got one week to find the right candidate for me to interview." He hung up.

I got to work. He interviewed the new candidate in less than a week, and he offered her the job. I continued to support that group, and leaders began to reach out to me independently for my perspective on issues.

Taking the opportunity to put my voice in the room had made a difference for the organization and strengthened my relationships with the leaders.

Using Your Authentic Voice

After recognizing the value of your authentic voice, it's important to use it. There are two steps that will help— letting go of your fear and embracing your value.

Letting Go of Fear

Finding your authentic voice and speaking up can be a challenge for anyone, from a woman in a frontline role to a CEO in the boardroom. Why? Humans seek validation. They want connections and to be part of a greater group.

When we speak our truth, it distinguishes us and separates us from the group. When our truth is new, diverges from the rest of the group, or represents a yet unheard-of perspective, we put our connections with others at risk. The group may now view us as somehow different, and perhaps, that difference does not fit with the group perspective. This fear of being different is even greater when no one else in the group looks like you or feels any affiliation to you.

To overcome this challenge, you need to feel a greater motivating force than fear. More importantly, you need to evaluate and understand the benefits of engaging with the group and connecting to others with your authentic voice. The benefits of speaking up are countless. As an individual, participating is likely to result in both personal and professional gains. Additionally, individuals in the room and the organization as a whole will benefit from your unique perspective. Without your voice, those gains could be lost.

Ask yourself: If I don't put my voice in the room, what do I lose? What does the team lose? What does the organization lose? Being true to yourself is important. Speaking up validates your value. It's your way of self-affirming that your perspective matters.

Embrace Your Value

Letting go of your fear allows you to embrace your true value. What you bring to the table is unique. You have a perspective to offer that cannot be replicated. When you ignore the opportunity to put your voice in the room, you are ignoring an opportunity to add value. Engaging with others should always be about transferring and increasing value.

By engaging and speaking with your authentic voice, you contribute value. Interestingly, this type of engagement also increases your value because, with each contribution, you generate more credibility, confidence, and momentum. For others, your engagement provides a different and valuable perspective. Whether your authentic perspective is embraced or not, you have provided a point of view that opens the aperture just a little wider for someone else and for better problem-solving.

Activate Your Purpose

Using your authentic voice activates your purpose. In this situation, you may have a multi-tiered purpose. Your specific organizational role defines one aspect of your purpose. It's what you've been hired to do. But your overall career purpose also has an impact. You have to consider why you do this work.

When you use your voice in your role or repeatedly in your career, you are putting your purpose into action. You use your voice to express your values, your purpose, your reason for contributing. Your voice opens the gateway for your purpose to be activated and realized.

Authenticity in Action

Sometimes we must dial into our purpose to find our value and our voice—even when speaking to those above our level.

Ms. T sat across from me at the small table in my office. She had a big meeting with the executive leadership team coming up to present the project she was leading. She wanted to work through the details to prepare. Her manager, one of the executive leadership team members, was in total support of the project yet had no funding for most of it. His strategy was to cut parts of the project and do as much as could be accomplished on the funding available.

Ms. T asked me, "I know I will be asked about risks for the project. It's underfunded, and I believe the funding should come from the executive team since the project benefits their organizations. I don't want to overstep my boss, but I have a strategy and plan that I think could work. I don't want to sit silent on this, but maybe I should respect his direction?"

"Tell me about your strategy," I asked. As she explained, it was clear that she was the expert on this project and had a thorough knowledge of how to execute the plan and to make the best use of funding.

"How can you discuss the funding needs without causing any negative ramifications for your boss? Doesn't he want this project executed, as well?" I asked.

"Yes, he wants to get this done," she said adamantly. "Maybe I should focus on the benefits to the enterprise and be clear about where the funding goes, then share that the project is underfunded right now and that one solution would be for the executive team to collectively provide funding?"

"You have the knowledge you need. What does the executive team, including your boss, expect of you in this role? What's your purpose?" I asked.

"I'm here to help the company achieve its targets and to execute the project," she replied.

"Can that be done if you stay silent on the risks?" I followed up.

"Point made and received," she said.

When we touched base a few days later after the meeting, Ms. T shared that she almost didn't bring up the funding issue since, due to time constraints, the group never even discussed risks to the project. However, right before the meeting ended, she was asked if there was anything she needed for the project. She took a deep breath and replied, "Money." Then, she began explaining her strategy to address underfunding.

She got support from one of the meeting leaders and was going to meet with her to discuss additional funding strategies.

"It was so hard to find my voice on this, but I'm so glad I did," she shared.

When you experience that feeling in the pit of your stomach telling you that your perspective is needed, be bold and put your voice in the room. You are enough. Do not question your value or capability. You are where you need to be.

That uncomfortable feeling is occurring because you specifically need to engage. It's urging you to use your voice. Push through your fear. Embrace your value. Activate your purpose. It may be the purpose of the role you are in at the time or your greater purpose for your authentic career. No matter how small or how great the opportunity, your authentic voice makes the difference.

Authenticity Lessons & Reflections

1. **Feel the fear and speak up anyway.** *When have you failed to put your voice in the room? How did you feel? What caused you to lose your voice?*

2. **Your authentic voice is powerful.** *What opportunities will you discover when using your voice to add value? How could you benefit professionally from being more engaged? What kinds of opportunities exist where you can be actively engaged and heard? How can you take advantage of your next opportunity?*

3. **Your voice benefits the team and the organization.** *How does your team benefit from your unique perspective? How can the organization benefit from your unique perspective right now? What unique value does your voice bring to the table?*

CHAPTER 12

A CLOSED MOUTH DOES NOT GET FED

Dear Authentic Women,

Let me debunk a myth for you on your quest to climb the corporate ladder: your work will not always speak for itself.

Being recognized for your value starts with you. It's not about waiting for others to connect your unique contributions to results. It's about you making that connection. Do you know how your authenticity drives results? How do you uniquely add value? How can you articulate the value you bring to your role?

Know your authentic value. Ask for what you've earned.

Tracy J

Women often struggle to ask for what they've earned. When your quest for what you earn is based on anything other than your authentic value, you won't be successful. You first need to understand the specific value you bring, and then you can get the value that you've earned. To do this, you must learn to elevate your approach.

I learned this when, after six months as the new chief diversity officer (CDO), I was frustrated and irritated. I was a direct report to the head of human resources, an executive vice president who reported to the CEO. All my peers who reported to the head of HR, except two, were vice presidents—a level above me. My work spanned the entire enterprise, while those peers focused on single, large segments of the business. Why wasn't I a vice president too?

I felt like my work spoke for itself. Over the past six months, my team had done some fabulous work. My leadership had made a difference, and I could list our accomplishments. As I mulled over our accomplishments and how I had developed as a leader, I started to list some talking points about why I deserved to be promoted. Late one fall afternoon, I summoned my courage and made an impromptu visit to my manager's office.

"Come in. Take a seat," he said. I sat down across from him. "What's up?" he asked as he sat down to focus on me.

"I want to be a vice president," I blurted out. "We have accomplished so much in six short months. I believe I should be at that level."

I saw the smile in his eyes before it crossed the rest of his face as he said, with a lighthearted laugh, "You don't do 25 percent of what a chief diversity officer of a Fortune 500 company does!"

Gut punch. I felt the wind expel from my lungs. What? He could see that I was shocked, so he continued more solemnly, "Check it out for yourself. Do the research. Find out what they do. You must have an enterprise-wide impact—deep and wide—and you need to reach outside the company to bring greater external visibility to our work and impact."

Stunned, I argued that I begged to differ on the 25 percent. "We do a lot," I said.

"Being busy does not mean being impactful," he said with a snort. Body slam! "Do your research," he reiterated.

"Okay. Fine. I'll take you up on that challenge," I said. "Please do," he responded. I stood and left.

I did the research and the work. He was right. There was more to being a CDO than what I was doing. I began to add value and focused on leading with a broader and deeper perspective that would be more visible outside the company. Our team expanded our reach and our accomplishments—having honest, compelling conversations with leaders across the enterprise.

I presented our work to the board, answering questions directly and with an honest perspective driven by my leadership and lived experience. My performance review came and went with a nice bonus but no promotion.

I stayed focused and put together a new diversity strategy for the enterprise and presented it to the CEO and his extended leadership team in early May of the following year. My thirty-minute presentation had to be distilled into fifteen minutes due to the meeting schedule. I brought my unique combination of humor and directness as I challenged the group to accelerate our work on hiring and developing diverse talent.

That challenge sparked open dialogue—and some conflict—among the group on how we could do better. I came back to my office after the presentation, relieved to have completed my first CEO presentation. People were getting real about the issues. That's what we needed: real talk. I had nailed it.

About an hour later, as I sat at my desk reviewing budget information, my boss appeared at my door. "Come on in," I said, anxious to hear the feedback from my presentation. Butterflies flew around in my stomach.

He took a seat across from me. "You did a great job presenting! I'm promoting you to vice president!" he said. "You've earned it."

"So now, I'm 100 percent CDO?" I quipped. He laughed. "I'll send you an email with the details. Good job today. Go celebrate!" He strode out of my office. I had brought my value to the table, and it was recognized.

Asking for Your Authentic Value

You must bring your authentic self to your role and recognize how your uniqueness creates results. This requires understanding the difference between accomplishing tasks and bringing value. You need to do more than a series of accomplishments. You must persevere until you discover how your unique contribution can bring value. When you understand this, opportunities for promotion or other recognition for your contributions will come.

Once you are clear about your authentic contributions, you're prepared to ask for the role, benefits, or recognition that is commensurate with your value.

Before you make the ask, use these three tips to prepare.

Elevate Your Perspective

When you start feeling that your role doesn't align with your value, you need to start thinking like your boss, the CEO, or the board of your company. What would make them undisputedly support your request for a promotion, job expansion, or more money? What are they looking for at the level above you or in an expanded role? Step into their shoes and walk around in them for a bit. Think about your request from all angles. What would your team say about your performance? What would your colleagues say? Your business partners? Be brutally honest with yourself. Seek feedback from your truth-tellers, sponsors, and others in your network.

Elevate Your Performance

Once you're clear about what's needed at the next level, it's time to elevate your performance to that level. Promotions are not all about accomplishments at the current level. They're about mastery and preparedness for the next level. While some leaders will promote based purely on potential, the potential must be demonstrated. Be thoughtful about what it takes to succeed at the next level. How have you grown or improved in your role? What skills have you acquired that make you ready for the next level? How are you already performing at the next level? It's not just about the results. It's about how you are getting work done. Talk to people who are at the level you seek to attain. Learn from them, then put your unique, authentic stamp on your work. Do what you do, like no one else can.

Elevate Your Effort

Focus your effort on more than completing tasks. Put additional effort into things that bring value to the organization and those that matter most for success in your desired next role. For example, as you rise higher in an organization, the ability to communicate your ideas to large groups, in order to share organizational goals and results, is a critical skill. Talk to others at the next level and observe their capabilities in this area.

View these new skills through the eyes of those who do it well to determine what you will need to focus on to develop and fine-tune those skills. Then, elevate your efforts by working harder and doing more to develop those skills. Make it your focus to be a visible, proactive communicator to your team and other parts of the organization to help prepare you for promotion.

Put additional, elevated effort on actions and behaviors that matter most in the next role. Persevere until you have closed the gap between where you are and where you want to be. Do the work.

Authenticity in Action

Asking for your value can be hard, but it's so much easier once you've elevated your perspective, performance, and effort. With these pieces in place, you have a strong platform for the discussion.

Ms. J sat across from me in my office. A single mother of two young children in a leadership role in a male-dominated field, she was tired. I always made sure I created a safe space where she could let down her defenses and speak freely about how she felt. She didn't need to keep her armor on during our coaching sessions.

"How are you?" I asked.

"Tired, but good. I feel like things are running smoothly on my team," she smiled tremulously. I waited for more. "I've worked really hard to get this team where it needs to be, but I am not recognized for it," she finished.

There it was.

"Tell me more about that," I probed. Over the past several months, we had worked together on how to structure her team, how to set goals and expectations, how to set personal boundaries, and how to clarify team issues. She did the work to address each of these opportunities, and it showed. She was an excellent leader and recognized as high-potential talent in the organization, but her frustration was palpable. She was operating at a higher level than her peers, and it seemed that no one, especially her boss, noticed.

The environment was tough. She was one of only a few women in the department and worked for a boss who never turned work off. He called at dinnertime. He texted late at night. He was ever-present in her life. She learned to manage his style by setting boundaries on when she would engage after leaving work. She clearly communicated her boundaries and still got the work done well.

Ms. J was the only woman on his leadership team. Although he would never acknowledge it, Ms. J was one of his go-to people. She picked up the slack on a multitude of things that her boss never realized she had done. She kept his head above water in many ways, but she was dying in this role because her value had expanded beyond the role and was not being properly recognized.

"I stay true to my values, opinions, and beliefs. I stick up for myself when necessary. I deliver on everything I commit to doing and more. But I'm not seen. Others get their promotions and opportunities but not me. I can't stay in this environment. It's not good for me," she said definitively. "I want an opportunity to grow. I want a promotion."

"So, what do you think about asking your boss for a promotion?" I suggested.

"I want to, but I don't feel that he would be open to it. And to be honest, I'm not sure I want to be in this environment anymore," she said.

"You've got options. You're talented. You can go for the promotion, look for another opportunity in the company, or you could leave. Let's work through both options," I suggested. We discussed how to start networking, tidying up her resume, and talking to HR and other leaders about new opportunities.

Over the next few meetings, we discussed asking for a promotion. We practiced what that conversation might look like. We went through her journey of elevating her performance. Ms. J was able to identify the ways that her leadership was adding value to her boss, her peers, and her team. She was able to articulate how she was already performing at the next level and what that value looked like. In a few weeks, she was ready to ask for the promotion.

The conversation with her boss was a tough one. As she covered the ways she added value and the new organizational structure she was putting forth that supported a promotion, her boss said skeptically, "I'll have to ask your business partners about your performance." Ms. J confidently replied, "Go ahead." All six of her business partners unanimously and overwhelmingly said she should be promoted. Her value could not be denied.

Having an authentic career includes making sure your value is recognized. Sometimes, others will see your value before you recognize it for yourself. At other times, those who should recognize your value never see it. The key is that you recognize your value, and you ask for what your value deserves. When you step up to ask for your value, make sure you elevate—perspective, performance, and effort. Focus your request on your unique value. When your request is based on your unique value and nothing else—not a long list of accomplishments or the desire to keep up with your peers—it's hard to deny.

Authenticity Lessons & Reflections

1. **Accomplishments are manifestations of your value.** *What accomplishments have you achieved? How has your authentic value driven those accomplishments? How can you share your accomplishments from the perspective of the unique value you added?*

2. **Own your value. Ask for what you want.** *When have you failed to ask for what your value supported? How did you feel? What needs to change for you to ask for your value in the future?*

3. **Persevere. Don't be deterred if it takes work to get where you want to go.** *What is the gap between where you are and where you want to be? What is the work to close the gap? What is your greatest growth opportunity towards your authenticity?*

CHAPTER 13

WHEN AUTHENTIC OPPORTUNITY CALLS

Your moment arrives when opportunity calls. Be ready. It's not always clear that it's an opportunity. Sometimes it's masked as a challenge. Sometimes it's masked as a change in role. Sometimes it's presented as a new job with a new company in a new state. It may even look like a demotion. Whatever disguise it wears, when it's your opportunity, your authenticity will help you see it for what it is: a unique opportunity that demands your unique brand of authenticity.

Creating an authentic career prepares you for these big authentic moments. Your authenticity creates an opportunity that you are uniquely prepared to handle. It's the moment that would not exist if you did not exist. It is uniquely yours, and it will fit like a glove when it arrives.

My Opportunity Moment

It was a short walk from the office to the hotel where I would present to the board of directors. This would be the first time the board would hear about the state of diversity and inclusion in the company, and it wasn't all pretty. I took several deep breaths as I ascended the escalator and headed into the meeting room. The room was filled with mostly white men, a couple of white women, one African American man, and two Latino men. I was the only African American woman and the only person with wild hair. I was wearing my naturally coily afro in all its red splendor!

This moment had been twenty-eight years in the making. Just two years earlier, I had been appointed as the company's chief diversity officer and had been unsure of how I could uniquely contribute to the role. I was not like the prior chief diversity officers. I had a deep operations background and lots of lived experience. My journey through human resources had given me the opportunity to coach many leaders and associates. I heard the stories of those women and people of color whose careers had been challenging and less than they had hoped they'd be.

I, too, had my experiences as an African American woman, and I knew there were facts behind the anecdotes. My operations background told me to dig into processes and data for answers. But before I jumped in and sanctioned a full study of diversity in the company, I ran the idea past a few close colleagues. While a couple supported my idea to take on the study, most told me to leave it alone. What would I do if the data showed there was a problem? Did I understand what I might be saying about the company? You're going to open a big can of worms that you can't close back up! While most of the advice was no, my authenticity told me to move ahead. This was my moment of truth, my big authentic moment. My biggest Wild Hair moment yet. Opportunity was calling for me to make a difference.

As I presented, my legs were shaking beneath me. This was my moment. I was pouring all my skill, my talent, my lived experience, and my entire authentic being into this moment. I would tell the people at the very top of this company that we needed to do better for women and people of color—better culturally, better in leadership development, better in hiring, just plain better. I knew that no one else could do that but me. It was my moment, and I owned it.

My authenticity had created opportunity, and I had answered the call. I received the board's endorsement for what would become a three-year journey that improved the representation of women and people of color in leadership.

Answering the Call

When opportunity comes calling in its best disguise, how do we know it's our big authentic moment? How do we know to answer the call? Apply your knowledge of yourself and your unique value to determine if the call is your opportunity.

Don't focus exclusively on the role, the title, the level, the benefits, or the challenges. Those are details that don't define you or determine your authentic value. Look beneath the surface and answer these questions:

1. *How am I uniquely prepared for this moment or opportunity?*
2. *How does this moment or opportunity align with my values?*
3. *How does this moment or opportunity connect to my purpose (i.e., my "why")?*

4. *How does this opportunity help me grow in authenticity and prepare me for what may be next?*
5. *How can this moment or opportunity help me to help others grow in their authenticity?*

When you answer these questions, if it feels that not pursuing the moment or the opportunity is a mistake, then you've found your answer. No matter what the opportunity looks like on the surface, it is something you must do. The surface may hold details that matter to some, but those details are not essential when building an authentic, successful career.

Authenticity in Action

When opportunity calls, it may not look like an opportunity on the surface. Identifying authentic opportunity is about discovering the question or the need beneath the surface and how you are the answer to the call.

I received a text message from a former colleague, Ms. W. She needed some coaching and advice, so we scheduled a conversation.

Ms. W was a force. She lived and breathed authenticity. She was outgoing, candid, confident, and eager to make a difference. She was confident in her capabilities and always spoke her mind. At times, she had felt confined in her roles, and she never really knew why. She was always authentic and impactful.

She got results by being herself, using every bit of her talent, experience, and skills. She never compromised herself. Those who didn't appreciate the force that she was simply didn't understand what it meant to be an authentic woman. She was 100 percent herself, 100 percent of the time. Admirable.

"I've got an opportunity to leave my company. The new opportunity is for a higher-level role at a much smaller private company. I'd be a big fish in a much smaller pond," she explained, "but I'd be responsible for all the functions in IT and report to the CEO." She was a woman of color working in IT, a rarity, with a chance to be in the C-suite.

"What excites you about this new smaller company? Why even consider the role?" I probed.

Ms. W had always aspired to the C-suite, where she could own the decisions that drive the company. She explained that this company was growing, and the culture was evolving. She could have a direct influence on the culture, especially for women. Someone from a board she sat on had recommended her. She had ignored the company's outreach, but the CEO was persistent after pursuing other candidates who didn't fit. After a dinner meeting, Ms. W had an offer.

"This makes life incredibly difficult, doesn't it?" I said. "You were doing just fine until someone wanted what you have to offer," I laughed.

"What's holding you back from jumping to take this job?" I asked.

"In some ways, it doesn't feel like an opportunity. It's the same pay. Fewer perks. Smaller organization. Smaller team. Less external visibility. A lesser-known company," she rattled off.

We continued talking, and she shared, with excitement, that she felt completely understood and accepted by the CEO. Her authenticity was valued. While on the surface this didn't look like an opportunity, underneath was a different story. Ms. W would be able to bring her unique experiences, skills, and talents to help shape an organization, giving her an opportunity to make a real difference for women. What she had, they needed. What she wanted, they craved. What she valued, they valued. It was a complete fit, but it didn't look like it on the surface.

"But is this your opportunity? What happens if you don't take this role? How will you feel?" I pushed.

"Like I missed something. Like something that was mine was given to someone else," she answered reflectively. That was her answer. She took the job, and she negotiated the pay and perks her authentic value commanded.

Creating an authentic career isn't easy. There are many times when the path isn't clear, or the answers aren't readily apparent. Being authentic is a choice. One that we make whenever we are challenged to know what is best for our career, our lives, and who we are. Whenever we make authentic choices, we grow. We add another milestone along our journey to our next authentic opportunity. With each new choice, our opportunities become greater, more impactful, more purposeful, and more meaningful, not just to ourselves but to others as well. It all starts by answering the call.

Over the course of your career and life, you will have many Wild Hair moments. To create the authentic career you love, in these moments, you must choose to be honest with yourself rather than allowing circumstances to dictate. You must choose to find your courage and not succumb to fear. You must choose to trust yourself, be confident, and not lose faith. You must choose to persevere and be resilient, to never give up. You must choose to own your authenticity and all it brings to the world.

You must choose you.

THANK YOU

Thank you for investing your time in reading my book. I hope you found something you could take from the stories, tips, and lessons. If so, be sure to share it with another woman who can benefit. We must pay our good fortune forward!

And don't hesitate to drop me a note, share your story, and tell me what you took away from this book. If you have suggestions, I'll take those too! I'd love to hear from you. Wild Hair Feedback (https://tracyjedmonds.com/wild-hair-feedback)

Tracy J

TracyJ@TracyJEdmonds.com
TracyJEdmonds.com
LinkedIn.com/in/TracyJEdmonds

ABOUT THE AUTHOR

Tracy J. Edmonds inspires those around her as a personal coach, diversity and inclusion consultant, and speaker. On a daily basis, she strives to encourage, affirm, and strengthen women leaders by helping them discover and own their leadership.

As a former corporate executive who climbed from the frontlines to chief diversity officer, Tracy is a highly sought-after coach and often-requested speaker. She blends her corporate and lived experience into her authentic brand of coaching and consulting.

Tracy's business savvy and strategic thinking capabilities help her clients achieve their most challenging personal, professional, and organizational goals. She grounds her approach in a strong belief that each individual's unique authenticity is capable of transforming themselves, a team, and an organization.

Tracy is currently enjoying her second career from her home in Carmel, Indiana, where she lives with her husband, three children, and her pugs. Read more and connect with Tracy at TracyJEdmonds.com.